Unholy Devotion:
Why Cults Lure Christians

Unholy Devotion

Why Cults Lure Christians

Harold L. Bussell
Foreword by Ronald Enroth

ZONDERVAN PUBLISHING HOUSE
of The Zondervan Corporation · Grand Rapids, Michigan

UNHOLY DEVOTION: Why Cults Lure Christians
Copyright © 1983 by The Zondervan Corporation

Scripture passages are quoted from *The Holy Bible: The New International Version,*
copyright © 1973, 1978 by the New York International Bible Society, unless otherwise indicated.

Designed by Ann Cherryman

Edited by Evelyn Bence and James E. Ruark

Library of Congress Cataloging in Publication Data
Bussell, Harold L.
    Unholy devotion.

    Bibliography: p.
    1. Cults—Controversial literature. 2. Christian sects—Controversial literature.
3. Christianity—20th century. 4. Christianity and culture. I. Title.
BL85.B93   1983   280'.09'04   82-21833
ISBN 0-310-37251-8

83 84 85 86 87 88 89   /   9 8 7 6 5 4

Printed in the United States of America

To my wife Carol
and children Monique and Bradford,
without whose encouragement
I would never have
finished this book

Contents

FOREWORD   9

PREFACE   11

1. THANK GOD I AM NOT ONE OF THEM
   —OR COULD I BE?   13

2. BUT YOU CAN SEE THE LOVE
   ON THEIR FACES   19

3. THE LORD LED ME   29

4. THEY EVEN SHARE THEIR BURDENS
   AND PRAY TOGETHER   41

5. BUT WE HAVE A NEW
   TESTAMENT CHURCH   51

6. YOU JUST HAVE TO HEAR
   OUR PASTOR!   61

7. BUT MORMONS DON'T DRINK
   OR SMOKE   73

8. THE PROBLEM OF PAIN   85

9. THE MANY PATHS TO SPIRITUALITY   99

10. PLEASE DON'T WATER THE GARDEN   111

NOTES   123

BIBLIOGRAPHY   126

Foreword

When most Evangelicals think of a cultist, the image that probably comes to mind is the persistent Jehovah's Witness at the front door or the brainwashed Moonie selling flowers on a street corner. We wonder how thinking people can ever be attracted to cultic groups whose teachings are so distant from biblical truths. We pity them for the spiritual darkness that envelops their lives.

As Christians we are smugly confident that they—the cultists—are far removed from our own world. Surely none of our friends or family would ever be tempted to get involved with such "crazy groups"! The jolting evidence presented in this book indicates otherwise. The primary objective of the author is to look at certain commonalities that cultists and Christians share. Before you conclude that such a suggestion is ridiculous or inappropriate, I recommend that you read this important book carefully.

Traditionally, Evangelical scholars have focused their attention on the heretical doctrines of cultic movements. Distinguishing false teaching from biblical truth should always be a primary concern of Christian cult-watchers. However, a unique aspect of Dr. Bussell's perspective is the assertion that evangelicals are seldom attracted to cults and aberrational Christian groups because of their doctrine; rather, the appeal is that basic human and spiritual needs are being met. Cults are successful because they promise what the author calls that elusive "something more." His point is that Christians are just as vulnerable as anyone else in reaching out for a perceived "spirituality."

I remember how startled I was to learn that a former student of mine had joined the Mormon church. Intellectually he knew that the teachings of that movement are contrary to Scripture. Yet there were certain overpowering personal needs in his life that were going unmet; he was offered the bosom of a family in the form of the Mormon church, and he succumbed. He had found a sense of community.

This book will disturb and threaten some readers. It will be difficult to escape the implication of the author's conclusion that cultic tendencies can be found in our own Evangelical backyard. For example, we need to hear what Dr. Bussell says about our vulnerability to destructive manipulation in some forms of group sharing so popular in evangelical (and cultic) circles. Those of us who have researched cults know how effectively they use guilt, fear, and spiritual intimidation to exploit people. This book illustrates how Christians often open themselves to similar exploitation.

In the course of my own research, I have talked with many Evangelical Christians who, for a variety of reasons, have become involved in a cult or aberrational Christian group after having made a commitment to Christ as Savior. Upon leaving the group, they have found the journey back to be painful, often lonely, and sometimes long. A common observation they have shared with me is the disappointment that few mainline Christians (including pastors) can comprehend how and why they were lured into a cult. As last I have a book that I can recommend which will explain clearly and powerfully why it can happen to *us*, not just to *them*.

—RONALD ENROTH
Westmont College
Santa Barbara, California

Preface

This book is not an attack on either cults or Christians. It is an examination of the things cultists and Christians hold in common. Many Christians assail the false teachings of the cults, but there are several dangers inherent in a one-sided approach to heretical teachings. First, we Christians may become blinded to the qualities we revere as signs of spirituality, and this, if not understood, can make us susceptible to cults.

Second, in our fight against deception and false teaching, we can easily attack people instead of problems and thus lose opportunities for ministry. We can also use our insights to excuse sinful pride, insensitivity, and lack of compassion.

God's Word calls us to think critically of the world in which we live and to discern the false teachings that seek to pull us off-center. There is a danger, however, of becoming critical, attacking people, blind to our own weaknesses and vulnerabilities. We must be careful lest we step over the fine line that changes us from critical thinkers into critical people.

I am concerned that we view the insights in this book through eyeglasses tinted with compassionate service to confused and hurting people who desperately need genuine concern and love.

The issues presented in these pages have been born in my own struggles and questions and from my relationships with many who have completed a painful, long, emotional, and fearful journey back to stability after being involved in a cult. All these people were raised in Evangelical homes and have returned to faith in Jesus Christ.

For simplicity I will use the word *cult* in this book to refer to any religious body that holds beliefs and practices clearly in opposition to historic Christianity as expressed in the Apostles' Creed.

My deepest thanks are due to those who encouraged and pushed me to write this book—my wife, Carol; Dr. Stanley Gaede; Norm Anderson; John Cox; and Arvin Engelson.

Chapter 1

Thank God I Am Not One of Them —or Could I Be?

What happened to John Moriconi? If it happened to him, could it happen to you?

John was an Evangelical Christian, a good Baptist. But then he spent eight years as a leader in the Children of God. Eight long years.

He left them. When I met him, he was a student at Gordon College, where I serve as Dean of the Chapel. Our long discussions of his past involvement with the Children of God and of his present search for God always left me thoroughly puzzled, yet fascinated. He had never wavered in his primary purpose: he sincerely desired to know God's truth and to relate personally to Jesus Christ. Yet his search had led him down a path that ended in the cultic community.

"How?" I wondered. "Why?"

John finally saw that the Children of God did not offer him the truth for which he longed. He has written a booklet entitled *Children of God, Family of Love,* and is the director of a ministry in Richmond, Virginia, that helps others who have followed the same path as he, for he realized (and he has shown me) that he is not alone in his misguided search.

We who sit on padded church pews may think that those "deluded, crazy cult members" are people who were previously unchurched pagans.

Many of them are, but let's look a little closer.

I counseled one young woman and over a period of time uncovered difficulties making decisions, troubles with severe depression, doubts concerning her faith, and an inability to cope with life. She related to me her background: raised in a prominent Evangelical church, knew the Scriptures, led Bible studies, had introduced many friends to Jesus Christ. But then her problems began. Her family became involved in an Evangelical community with cultic leanings. They were not alone in their decision, as many members of their church, including the pastor, joined the questionable group. They sold their homes. They dropped close friends. Eventually children were separated from their parents and reared by "more spiritual" parents. In group sessions, individuals were pressured publicly to confess attitudes, sexual fantasies, and past sins.

For this young woman, these years were full of confusion, pain, and hurts that caused her journey back to stability to be long and treacherous.

Three other Christians, the mother and two sisters of Akiko Lrick, joined a Korean cult. At a church conference in upstate New York, Akiko told me about her family in Japan. Her mother and sisters had been active for years in a Japanese Evangelical church. Later she wrote to me,

> ... My sisters in their music college days were active in Campus Crusade. They were both promising students in the two most reputable music schools in Japan. Then all of a sudden they found a "better way" to dedicate more totally to the "promise" of eradicating the sinful nature. They clearly believe they can achieve sinless states here and now following the Moon recipe for salvation—gaining three men and three women converts to start with, for that is a major ingredient among others—and that their offspring are born without sinful natures for the parents are Moonies and married by the dictate of Mr. Moon. They were married to their men not knowing even the names of their future husbands in mass weddings of three thousands couples at once!! in Seoul, Korea, some seven years ago. They have been in this movement for a good twelve years now.
>
> Five years ago they had a huge expensive one week retreat for the family—nonbelievers—in Honolulu, to which I was enticed. But, when unconverted even after that, I was found "dead" by my sisters and to a lamentable degree by my mother.

These three women were searching for fellowship and an answer to the problem of sin. Where did they end up? As active leaders in the Unification Church.

In January 1981, I met an acquaintance whom I hadn't seen for more than ten years. He told me that his wife, raised in an Assemblies of God missionary's home, had for a time been an active member of the People's Temple led by the Reverend Jim Jones.

I am sure many pastors could draw from their journals similar accounts and stories. They have no doubt faced the same questions and confusions as I: Why are *we* prey to cults?

Most available books, workshops, and seminars on cults are built around a we/they mentality that contrasts their heretical doctrines against the biblical truths on which we stand. Until recently even my own focus has been on the error and corruption of their teachings.

But are other issues involved?

In all my discussions with people allured by cults, I have talked to only one person whose attraction centered on doctrine. Because doctrine was so seldom mentioned, I was forced to reexamine my past discussions and ask whether or not Evangelicals are particularly susceptible to cults.

After much thought, reflection, and discussion, I faced the evidence: Yes, as Evangelicals we *are* vulnerable.

I looked back on my fifteen years of ministry in California, Europe, and New England, and I reconstructed my conversations with those who had come out of a cult, had family members in cults, or were attending cult groups out of curiosity. Definite and similar patterns of thought kept recurring, as steadily as a ticking metronome. Evangelicals do have something in common with cults: zeal and confidence. We cherish and value similar signs of spirituality. Many of us share with them similar ideas concerning authority, loyalty, and submission.

A close examination of popular Western cults reveals that many began in an Evangelical church or under leaders who claimed Christianity—men and women from solid church backgrounds.

Sun Myung Moon, founder of the Unification Church, was reared in a Presbyterian home. Jim Jones, founder of the People's Temple, at one time attended a Nazarene church; later he pastored an interdenominational church and a Disciples of Christ congregation. Moses David (David Berg), founder of the Children of God, is the son of Evangelical parents, served as a minister in a Christian and Missionary Alliance church, and was involved for a time in a Christian television ministry. Victor Paul Wierwille, founder of The Way, came out of the Reformed Church, where he served as pastor to a number of active congregations; during the forties he served as an adjunct professor of New Testament at a leading Evangelical college.

While it is easy and comfortable for us to think in terms of "them" and "us"—being thankful that we are not one of them—the fact is that many of them *used to be* one with us. Might we Christians be more myopic than we realize? Might we need to expand our field of vision and note that our sense of security and offensive attacks on their doctrines are blinding us? It is time we read carefully the fine print of past decades.

Many of the white woodframe churches that dot the New England countryside are Unitarian. At one time in their history almost all these churches were Trinitarian, biblical, and parishes of Congregational, Baptist, or Episcopal denominations.

Mary Baker Eddy, founder of the Christian Scientists, and Charles Taze Russell, founder of the Jehovah's Witnesses, were both raised in markedly Christian homes and churches.

In our fervor to point out errors of doctrine, we have virtually ignored our own shortcomings and vulnerabilities. Remember, former Evangelicals died in Jonestown and currently are active in the Unification Church, The Way, the Children of God, and other heretical groups.

It is easy for us, as churches and as individuals, to put on our doctrinal sunglasses and squint our eyes so as to block these issues from our sight. But in doing so, we only remove the reminder of our responsibility to face our own susceptibility to cultic deception.

Perhaps we should pray that God will give us full sight and remove our arrogant attitudes. Too many of our soldiers have fallen for us to feel that our battlelines are so impenetrable. The fallen *could* be one of us.

QUESTIONS FOR DISCUSSION

1. Do you know people who have been drawn to cults or have come out of a cult? What were the reasons for their involvement?
2. In light of this chapter, what are your reactions to Matthew 24:22–24? (See also Mark 13:20–22.)

> "If those days had not been cut short, no one would survive, but for the sake of the elect those days will be shortened. At that time if anyone says to you, 'Look, here is the Christ!' or, 'There he is!' do not believe it. For false Christs and false prophets will appear and perform great signs and miracles to deceive even the elect—if that were possible."

3. When you think about cults, do you only contrast them with your faith or do you compare your similarities? Why and how?
4. What questions has this chapter raised in your mind? Do you agree or disagree with the concepts presented? Why?

Chapter 2

But You Can See the Love on Their Faces

"I've found new life. Joy. Happiness. Purpose. Love."

"I've given up my drug habit. My immorality. My old sinful habits."

Such testimonies are frequently touted by Christians: "Because we have experienced, we know." But we are far from alone in our assurances. Cult members also boast of changed lives and spiritual trophies.

Our emphasis on subjective religious experience has caused many secular observers to confuse Evangelicals with other "radical" religious groups who also exhibit changed lives, testimonies of joy, smiling faces, and evangelistic zeal.

Our overemphasis on subjective experience has some of its roots in our strong reaction against the rationalism, naturalism, and liberalism that has infiltrated many Protestant denominations over the past decades. For the many people who lacked an in-depth personal apologetic, verification of their faith became a matter of subjective and experiential witness. We felt good all over when someone announced, "I'm not prepared to argue doctrine. All I know is I am a *new* person." Such a safe retreat could not be challenged intellectually.

But is this sort of defense really safe? Many of the gospel songs written during the last four or five decades reflect the importance placed on this subjective approach to faith and life. A perfect and familiar example is a line from "He Lives" by Alfred H. Ackley: "You ask me how I know He lives? He lives within my heart." But we are facing cults who use these same terms. They boast of their results, speak of changed lives, even sing these same gospel songs.

Several years ago I curiously watched a Sunday morning gospel television program filmed in Florida. The music was moving and well-presented. The stories were challenging. One young person's inspiring testimony encouraged others to accept Christ, the giver of happiness, joy, and peace. Wanting to see what the other channels presented, I turned the dial. To my surprise, I saw and heard former antiwar activist Rennie Davis sharing almost the same testimony. He claimed he had found the truth, accompanied by unbelievable peace and joy. He saw that his sixties' search really had been a hunger and thirst for a deeper spiritual life. He was now clean-shaven, wearing a stylish suit, and beamed a smile similar to the student on the other program. He even promised the viewer the same fulfilled life.

Spiritually I was deeply moved while listening to his tale of transformation from a life of drugs and angry activism. But as he drew his remarks to a close, I could hardly believe what I was hearing. He encouraged the audience to contact a local meditation group and there find the same peace, joy, and spiritual blessings he had discovered. I hated to admit it, but until the "sponsor" of the program was identified, I could tell no difference between the attitudes, promised results, or quality and genuineness of conversion of the two speakers.

I know many people who have attended est seminars or encounter groups or have converted to cults and who have experienced moral and positive character changes similar to yours or mine. But does "similar" mean "the same as"?

Of course not. Let's look at what really happens to these people.

THE BIG DIFFERENCE—THE GOSPEL

As Christians we often bear witness to the *results* of the gospel rather than to the gospel itself. To do so exclusively is a serious mistake, for it is amazingly easy to confuse various ideological conversion experiences with the true new birth.

Many people undergo dramatic experiences as they are converted to est, an encounter group, a meditation group, Marxism, or a cultic religious community. All conversion experiences offer common psychological results. The discovery of a "new life" or a new system for belief gives a fresh reason for living and an exciting focus for life. A new sense of emotional security is born, and its breath is full of direction, a sense of belonging, and often happiness.

But the new birth that is believed and known in the historic church is a result of the work of the Spirit of God who enables us to acknowledge our sins and confess Jesus Christ as Lord. The new birth is not based on feelings, but on our coming into union with the resurrected Christ—not just *any* Christ, but He who is God and man at once.

Feelings that accompany conversion to Jesus Christ may be positive *or* negative. To the rich, young ruler who turned away from Christ (Luke 18:18–29), the results of conversion looked negative and costly. Jesus asked that he leave his materialistic god, his personal possessions.

Frequently we stretch the biblical data to state that the results of true conversion to Christ will all be positive, that our salvation will be accompanied by astounding personal success. In high school I attended a youth rally in Sacramento, California, in which the guest speaker was a recently converted national beauty queen. In her testimony she attributed all of her success to her faith in Jesus Christ. I then wondered if her conversion was the only reason for her success. During her talk I repeatedly rememberd her vital statistics, which had been printed in the previous week's *Sacramento Bee*. Had they not been a factor?

What about the other Christians in the contest? Did they lack faith, or bustlines?

I had brought a nonbelieving friend to the meeting in hopes of introducing her to Christ. She was about ninety pounds overweight and was convinced she was dying of terminal acne. During the testimony she quietly whispered to me, "If I accept Christ, do you think He would help me become a beauty queen?"

Our testimonies cannot only confuse seekers, but can also lay tremendous guilt on people who can't live up to the ideal Christian model set before them. Stories are often punctuated with successes and promises that all problems will be resolved as easily and quickly as the Waltons' on TV.

How do we sort out the differences between a witness such as Rennie Davis and the young person on the gospel program? How do we separate the promises of success from the realities of living in a fallen world? Were the witnesses of the young woman on the television program and the converted beauty queen really the gospel? If *results* in our lives or our hearts are the gospel, then Rennie Davis's experience with meditation is also the gospel, because the criterion is change instead of Christ. This is a most confusing matter for us Christians. Continually I meet believers who condemn themselves because their experience of Christ doesn't seem quite as vibrant or successful as someone else's.

Do you ever wonder if you are useless to God because you have no great spiritual experience about which you can boast? Do you ever feel like a second-class Christian because you have some difficult habit, sin, or problem you can't overcome? If so, you may be susceptible to a cult that will promise you "results." Cults *always* offer that something more that seems to be lacking.

Perhaps contemporary Christian biographies are so popular because they are exciting and carry with them secrets on how to fulfill our unrealistic expectations of what conversion should be. Many books of this kind give glowing reports of clean slates and new hearts before or instead of a holistic and scriptural picture of Jesus Christ and His church.

Biblical believers struggled with their lives, imperfections, and even failures. David, a great leader used by God, had moral problems and difficulties as a father at various times. Moses was called by God, but still fought with his flaring temper. Paul and Peter had a disagreement over Peter's following the Galatians away from the gospel. Paul, Mark, and

Barnabas parted ways because of differences. God's Word presents a larger picture than we often allow ourselves to see. Hebrews 11, the great Faith Chapter, does not talk of faith in the context of "success." It says that many "by faith" were beaten, stoned, sawn in half, tempted, afflicted, and socially rejected.

TESTIMONIES ARE NOT THE GOSPEL

The testimonies of the young woman on the television program and the beauty queen were not the gospel.

Matthew 3:2 says: "Repent, for the kingdom of heaven is near." Jesus Christ entered human history in the Incarnation, lived, died, and rose from the dead so that we might enter that kingdom. The Lord Jesus promised, "Whoever believes and is baptized will be saved" (Mark 16:16). When we, through trust, are thus brought into union with Christ our Savior, we can stand totally forgiven and justified before a righteous and holy God. We take our place in His church, where we can be nourished and built up in the faith. The results felt or seen after true new birth vary considerably among individuals, and they must not be presented as the gospel. God's work by the Holy Spirit in me differs from His work in my fellow Christian. There are a variety of gifts and effects. For in Christ, we will be led into the change of heart that results from conversion —in fact, conversion means change. But we must remember that these changes are not the gospel. The gospel is something objective and outside of us—complete and finished in Jesus Christ. The gospel is not established by our feelings, moods, or changes, however valid they may be.

When we confuse the results with the message, we tend to remove the basis of Christian living from faith in Christ. Guilt then creeps in and pushes us to compare ourselves with the most current religious hero. Karl Marx once said, "The Christian world is only a reflection of the real world." Perhaps he understood us better than we do.

Often we dress up the latest fad and attach Bible verses to it. In the fifties the secular cry was for light-hearted fun, Ivy League clothes, and happy times. Ours was the "abundant life in Jesus." The sixties called for social revolution: Evangelical books and posters soon boasted of titles like *Jesus the Revolutionary*. The culture of the seventies turned to T-groups and psychological encounter cells; of course, we "discovered" relational theology. However, it is devastating when we insist on living at the reflective edge of culture in the area of experience.

Consider this: Beauty queens and athletes were the attractive Christian flag-bearers of the fifties. In the sixties the spotlight turned to converted activists, in the seventies to transformed drug addicts, and now again to sports figures and entertainers. If we continue on this path of trendy Christianity and pop religion, we will keep on evoking tremendous insecurity among "normal" Christians who feel their experience of Jesus Christ is inadequate. These people are then tempted to run to a cult for help.

In contrast to modern testimonies, let us look at conversion and faith in several biblical accounts. I think first of the dialogue between Christ and His disciples when He entrusted them with power to perform great miracles.

> The seventy-two returned with joy and said, "Lord, even the demons submit to us in your name."
>
> He replied, "I saw Satan fall like lightning from heaven. I have given you authority to trample on snakes and scorpions and to overcome all the power of the enemy; nothing will harm you. However, do not rejoice that the spirits submit to you, but rejoice that your names are written in heaven" (Luke 10:17–20).

The lesson is so very clear. The Lord Jesus encouraged His disciples to rejoice, not in the spectacular results of an authoritative ministry, but rather in the good news that they had been accepted by the mercy of God. In Scripture, conversion experiences and responses to the gospel vary. Paul experienced a dramatic conversion.

> As he neared Damascus on his journey, suddenly a light from heaven flashed around him. He fell to the ground and heard a voice say to him, "Saul, Saul, why do you persecute me?"
>
> "Who are you, Lord?" Saul asked.
>
> "I am Jesus, whom you are persecuting," he replied. . . .

Then Ananias went to the house and entered it. Placing his hands on Saul, he said, "Brother Saul, the Lord—Jesus, who appeared to you on the road as you were coming here—has sent me so that you may see again and be filled with the Holy Spirit." Immediately, something like scales fell from Saul's eyes, and he could see again (Acts 9:3–5, 17–18).

For Paul the change was dramatic. But by contrast, Timothy grew gradually into the faith through family instruction.

I have been reminded of your sincere faith, which first lived in your grandmother Lois and in your mother Eunice and, I am persuaded, now lives in you also (2 Tim. 1:5).

EARLY LEADERS NEVER CONFUSED CONVERSION AND REBIRTH

On Pentecost, Peter made sure that accounts of conversion and saving faith were connected directly to the message of the gospel, although he affirmed the experiential response of the people as a gift from God. After Pentecost he did not encourage people to follow Christ for the experiential benefits He gave. Instead Peter preached the historical, crucified, and resurrected Christ.

"'In the last days, God says,
I will pour out my Spirit on all people.
Your sons and daughters will prophesy,
your young men will see visions,
your old men will dream dreams.
Even on my servants, both men and women,
I will pour out my Spirit in those days,
and they will prophesy.
I will show wonders in the heaven above
and signs on the earth below,
blood and fire and billows of smoke.
The sun will be turned to darkness
and the moon to blood
before the coming of the great and
glorious day of the Lord.
And everyone who calls
on the name of the Lord will be saved.'

"Men of Israel, listen to this: Jesus of Nazareth was a man accredited by God to you by miracles, wonders and signs, which God did among you through him, as you yourselves know. This man was handed over to you by God's set purpose and foreknowledge; and you, with the help of wicked men, put him to death by nailing him to the cross. But God raised him from the dead, freeing him from the agony of death, because it was impossible for death to keep its hold on him. . . .

"Therefore, let all Israel be assured of this: God has made this Jesus, whom you crucified, both Lord and Christ" (Acts 2:17–24, 36).

When Peter clearly preached Christ, the crowd responded by asking, "What shall we do?" (v. 37). Peter responded,

"Repent and be baptized, every one of you, in the name of Jesus Christ so that your sins may be forgiven. And you will receive the gift of the Holy Spirit. The promise is for you and your children and for all who are far off—for all whom the Lord our God will call" (vv. 38–39).

Peter was not satisfied to give witness only to the experience itself. He affirmed the miraculous, but preached the gospel of Jesus Christ as his basis for calling his listeners to repentance.

The same pattern ensued in Acts 3. When Peter and John healed a beggar at the temple gate, the onlooking crowd grew curious and excited. They wanted to set Peter and John on spiritual pedestals. The crowd claimed the apostles were wonder-workers. But instead of preaching miracles—or strategies for evangelism and global renewal—Peter and John continued to preach Jesus Christ, crucified and resurrected. Their message called their listeners to reality—to a true life found through repentance and belief in the work and person of Jesus Christ.

Repentance does not always result in external happiness, joy, and success, but it does bring a confidence that allows us to face and obey God's will through the grace received in Jesus Christ. Conversion also prompts a change of lifestyle, a new system of ethics, and often a painful death to sin. But confusing these joys or trials with the gospel can be devastating to even the serious believer. The gospel of experience will not keep us and deliver us on a life-long basis. When people who have become Christians for the benefits it will bring them make this discovery, they are prey to the zealous cults that promise better experiences and share greater testimonies.

The gospel, then, is based solely on the objective work of Jesus Christ. The great mystery of the faith is that Christ has died, Christ is risen, Christ will come again. The biblical pattern and model shows that we should preach Christ, not the gospel of varying results.

FOUNDATION FOR FREEDOM

Christ's work frees us from comparative Christianity. It protects us from the sin of spiritual navel-gazing. In the church we can face sin, deal with it properly before God, and call for obedience. Faith in Christ gives us the Holy Spirit, who enables us with His power to face, work through, and grow in the midst of our problems. The gospel protects us from having always to look for that elusive "something more," which cults unhesitatingly promise to the burdened believer.

QUESTIONS FOR DISCUSSION

1. Have you found the clarification between the gospel and results of conversion helpful? If so, why?
2. When you discuss your faith with others, do you tend to confuse the gospel with your response to the gospel?
3. Have you ever been confused by the positive witness of one who has been converted to a cult? If so, how has this chapter helped you understand why?

Chapter 3

The Lord Led Me

"The Lord led me."

"I felt led of the Lord."

Have you ever spoken or heard such phrases? What is your reaction to hearing them? Inwardly do you ever question their validity?

Many Christians are easily manipulated by anything that hints of spirituality. And who can be more spiritual than an enthusiastic member of a cult?

In his book *Youth, Brainwashing and the Extremist Cults*, Ronald Enroth says, "Most cult groups display great skill in using biblical language and Christian terminology. Even Eastern religious cults appeal to the Bible for support and affirmation by a selective use of texts that fit their own systems."[1] Also, "Basic to the biblical view of God's adversary is the fact that he claims to be very religious."[2]

Mary Baker Eddy claimed to have new spiritual insights and used the Bible as the foundation for Christian Scientism. The Jehovah's Witnesses also use Scripture as their authority. Observe the extent of the spiritual appeal in the following letter written by Karen Layton, personal secretary to Jim Jones:

> Special blessings come to those who honor the work of God with their offerings. In recent meetings there has been a revelation about obedi-

ence offerings of certain amounts. . . . God will also reveal to Pastor Jones what your obedience offering should be.[3]

"But he was a cult leader," you say. Yes, but ask yourself how often you have said, "The Lord led me." It sounds spiritual, but nearly every cult touts this phrase or an equivalent.

When we as Evangelicals couple this phrase with a definition of spirituality based on frequency and fervor of devotions, quiet time, prayer, evangelism, and Bible study or on sheer subjective emotion, we are wide open to manipulation and deception by cults that define spirituality in similar terms. We can easily become confused about who is spiritual and who isn't.

A BIBLICAL PHRASE?

We frequently fail to question and challenge leaders who present "new" spiritual insights or truths or who claim to be led of the Lord. Perhaps we fail to challenge our own use or misuse of the phrase "The Lord led me."

In reality, God does lead us. God's direction is clearly evident throughout Scripture and history, throughout even our individual, private histories. However, "The Lord led me" *can* be a cover-up, disguising our own desires, irresponsibility, and attempts at manipulation. What an easy way to avoid responsibility for making the decisions continually placed before us! A misuse of this phrase can easily border on taking God's name in vain.

At first glance the phrase sounds quite spiritual, but a close examination of Scripture reveals that it is not always biblical. On several occasions the phrase is used by or to describe false prophets or deceptive people. Jacob deceived his father by spiritualizing issues. Esau, Jacob's brother, had just gone hunting. Too quickly, it seemed, Jacob, claiming to be Esau, brought the killed game to his father. "How did you find game so quickly?" Isaac asked. Having usurped Esau's place, Jacob lied to his sick, blind father. But notice Jacob's very "spiritual" response: "The LORD your God gave me success" (Gen. 27:20).

Jacob was playing dangerous games, spiritualizing in order

to manipulate someone he knew would believe such words. Jacob wasn't a false cult leader or prophet; he was God's own chosen servant.

The Gibeonites tried this same tactic on Joshua. Joshua and his army had destroyed the city of Ai, and the Gibeonites feared they were next. To deceive Joshua, they dressed up as if they had traveled from a far country. When they came face to face with Joshua, they spiritualized issues to manipulate him: "Joshua asked, 'Who are you and where do you come from?' They answered: 'Your servants have come from a very distant country because of the fame of the LORD your God'" (Josh. 9:8–9).

Joshua bit at their line baited with "spiritualese" and he was hooked. He immediately made a treaty with them. Joshua and Isaac, both leaders chosen by God, were deceived by spiritual talk.

Leaders were not the only biblical characters deceived by such language. Jeremiah cried out God's displeasure with His people who followed the ones blindly claiming, "Thus saith the Lord."

> Then the LORD said to me, "The prophets are prophesying lies in my name. . . . They are prophesying to you . . . delusions of their own minds" (Jer. 14:14).

> "I have heard what the prophets say who prophesy lies in my name. They say, 'I had a dream! I had a dream!'" (Jer. 23:25).

Time has not strengthened our Achilles' heel. The deception of God's people by those who "spiritualize" always has been and will be with us. It sounds so right, yet the deception is so subtle. We may not be using God as an excuse for a lie, as was Jacob; we may simply be deceiving ourselves, thinking God endorses our own fabrications. My employer, Gordon College, is located on the picturesque and historic north shore of Boston—perhaps one of the most scenic areas in the United States, especially in the fall. One spring I received more than twenty letters from leaders of musical groups, pastors, and evangelists who had been "led of the Lord" to minister to our students during the first two weeks of October. Why, I wondered, doesn't God ever seem to lead ministries to New England during February? Either we should cancel classes for a week and hold twenty chapel services or the Holy Spirit is confused or someone has bad hearing.

Almost all cult leaders place a high emphasis on being "led by the Lord." When we misuse this term, we can easily make ourselves prey to cults or churches moving in cultic directions.

Stephen B. Clark describes in his book *Man and Woman in Christ* how some people justify their hidden agendas: "I am trying to be led by the Spirit, and the Spirit has not led me to adopt the kind of position that scripture seems to teach."[4]
This approach is not commonly represented in scholarly literature, but can be heard among Christians at large. You will notice that the "spiritual" is placed above the authority of the Word. Clark states, "The statement . . . 'led by the Spirit' can be a way to bypass scriptural authority. This happens when someone makes the Spirit's leading the decisive factor in accepting anything as true. When such people say they are 'waiting for the Spirit's leading,' they are saying that they personally require direct revelation or inspiration in order to accept something as true. . . . It would be a mistake, they feel, to pattern our lives on the way he was leading a group of Christians 2000 years ago. Such a position does not deny outright the authority of scripture, but it does amount to such a denial in practice."[5]

Charles Farah, Jr., of Oral Roberts University tells the story of a young Evangelical who carried this framework of thinking to its logical conclusion: "I don't read my Bible anymore," the young man said. "I don't have to read my Bible devotionally anymore, because I get mine direct."[6] This young man has discovered no new tricks. He offers a clear picture of the sentiments of the false teachers who challenged both Old and New Testament leaders.

In the first century those who thought that personal revelation was an authority above Scriptures were called Gnostics. The idea is dispelled by Peter in his second letter: "Grace and peace be yours in abundance through the knowledge of God and of Jesus our Lord" (2 Peter 1:2).

Peter does not point to or single out some Christian's superior leading. He addresses all Christians as having real knowledge of Christ. It is the same kind of holistic, non-Gnostic knowledge to which Paul refers in 1 Corinthians 2:12, 14.[7]

We must ever guard ourselves against the words and pet phrases that hint of superior spirituality.

OPEN AND SHUT DOORS

What both Christian groups and cults call "the open-door policy" is another dangerous spiritualization. Both sectors frequently refer to "God's shutting (or opening) the door."

Right from the start, let me make my position clear. God does open and close doors. I have seen evidence of this in my life, and I am sure you have in yours. It is encouraging to reflect on our lives and remember the times God has indeed shut or opened doors. Such memories build our faith. The danger, however, is to view all lost opportunities as shut doors. The convenient phrase "God closed the door" can be a variation on the tune previously mentioned: manipulation, avoiding responsibility, and self-justification.

While I was speaking in the Southwest one time, a young Christian in deep distress asked me if we could discuss his losing his job. It was clear that he had been irresponsible in establishing priorities, was undisciplined, and had been fired as a result. After a long discussion, he concluded, "I guess God must be shutting the door for me here."

I don't agree.

God does shut doors, of course. Since that discussion, however, I have been asking myself whether Christians use this phrase too freely. Do we use the phrase as another set of spiritual buzzwords to avoid responsibility or to cover up a fear of going through an open door of opportunity? Do we say "God has shut the door" when the lost opportunity is really a result of our own failure?

In Scripture, the closed-door policy is pictured in two ways. The Bible is full of accounts in which God in His divine guidance closed doors to redirect the lives of people who trusted in

Him. However, Scripture also couples the shut-door policy
with the sin of neglect.

Remember the parable of the ten virgins? The story implies
faith, morality, and virtue on the part of all ten virgins. But
some were foolish. When the hour of the wedding arrived, they
did not take the opportunity to provide sufficient fuel. In one
moment the door shut and their opportunity passed.

Their lack of oil was a result of doing nothing. Jesus attributed no serious evil or sin to them; they were simply indiffer-
ent to opportunities before them. They saw a door shut because of neglect—just like the young man who lost his job.
They followed the shut-door policy, and Christ labeled them
"foolish"—not spiritually alert.

The use of the phrase "God shut the door" may reveal more
about neglect than spirituality. "How shall we escape if we
ignore such a great salvation?" (Heb. 2:3). "Do not forget to
entertain strangers. . . . Do not forget to do good and to share
with others, for with such sacrifices God is pleased" (Heb.
13:2, 16).

White clapboard New England homes become dark, de-
caying buildings with time and neglect. Failure to put fuel in a
jet will never get the plane or its passengers to the desired
destination. We don't have to choose evil or willfully sin to
spoil our character—neglect alone is sufficient.

Closed doors may be the result of good things left undone.
No evil was attributed to the travelers who passed by the
wounded man on the road to Jericho; they simply passed by.
On Judgment Day there will be much talk of "closed doors,"
but the meaning of the phrase will then be different from our
usual intent. It will be used in regard to empty lamps, buried
talents, tasteless salt, and deeds left undone.

God's Word challenges us to walk through the open doors
set before us and to perform good works. If a door is shut, we
must not be too quick to attribute the blockage to God. We
need to see all these easy-answer phrases in their biblical context. Only when we see the total picture are we protected from
self-deception and a lopsided Christianity that is a dangerous
cultic look-alike.

NIGHT-SHIFT CHRISTIANITY

What is at the root of Christian groups who spiritualize issues to justify their lifestyle and service to God? Could it be a truncated view of the work of the Holy Spirit?

We have limited the work of God's Spirit to small aspects of our lives, those we term "spiritual."

I once had a fascinating discussion with a man whom God has placed in a strategic position of international leadership. Decisions made by his company affect families, nations, and the needy world-wide. The man is a sincere Christian and exhibits an honest desire to live according to God's way. I was pleased that our conversation turned to spiritual matters, but I was puzzled when he said, "I admire men like you who have received a call into full-time Christian service. I have always wanted to be in full-time Christian work."

What a tragedy, I thought. He made such a distinction between my work and his. He saw "the ministry" as a higher calling than his own. He saw his job—and the jobs of others in the "secular" workplace—as ordinary or perhaps God's second best.

I saw his life in a perspective different from his. All life is to be under the lordship of Christ. Every Christian's life is a ministry. Decisions made by this man's company have global impact. How unfortunate (and unbiblical) that he couldn't view the influence he had as an open door of opportunity to bring his total life under the lordship of Christ, as an open door to his ministry.

I have come to realize that this man is not alone in his view of himself as a second-class Christian. Many Christians live under similar clouds of uselessness, feeling as though they have God's second best because they are not in "full-time" Christian work. Such feelings and the guilt that accompanies them make laypeople susceptible to cults and manipulators who beg for commitments to or promise opportunities for full-time service.

James and Marcia Rudin state, in their book *Prison or Paradise?*, "Cult followers often work full time for the group. They work very long hours, for little or no pay."[8]

Most cults, like many Evangelicals, divide time and activities into two categories: the sacred and the secular. Michael Griffiths describes this situation: "Thus, part of our life is spent 'spiritually'—at innumerable meetings, in personal prayer and Bible reading, in public worship and in 'profitable' conversation with men about their souls. The rest of our time, however, must, perforce, be spent in a less worthy way on 'the things of this world'—eating, drinking, sleeping, working, playing, being with our families, digging in the garden, having holidays and so forth."[9]

We overlook the scriptural teaching that God has ordained all these "secular" activities and therefore must have some intention in them. Scripture regards everything we do as part of our Christian walk. Dividing existence into narrow, compact divisions dissolves the practical delights of a satisfied, effective, and fulfilled life in Jesus Christ. The instruction of Scripture is remarkably vivid and unclouded and cannot easily be spiritualized: "So whether you eat or drink or whatever you do, do it all for the glory of God" (1 Cor. 10:31).

Relaxation, for example, was an integral part of the spiritual life of Jesus Christ: "Then, because so many people were coming and going that they did not even have a chance to eat, he said to them, 'Come with me by yourselves to a quiet place and get some rest.' So they went away by themselves in a boat to a solitary place" (Mark 6:31–32).

CHRIST NEGATES SIN, NOT HUMANITY

Christ came to negate sin, not our humanity. Jesus Christ seeks to redeem us from our sins, not from relaxation, work, fulfillment in life, and food consumption.

Paul echoes the theme of our humanness. He invites us to think about and examine *all* of life, not simply one "spiritual" division or one segment we label as "spirituality." "Finally, brothers, whatever is true, whatever is noble, whatever is right, whatever is pure, whatever is lovely, whatever is admirable—if anything is excellent or praiseworthy—think about such things. . . . And the God of peace will be with you" (Phil. 4:8–9).

Paul does not insult our intelligence by telling us what is pure or by assigning purity to our "spiritual" compartment of life. Paul presents an expansive, wide-open invitation that activates our minds to be fully involved in the totality of life. The words *whatever* and *anything* invite us to discover all God has created. Sanctification is not the development of one spiritual aspect of reality; it involves doing everything, living every minute creatively and obediently to the glory of God.

In his letter to the Ephesians, Paul addresses various issues of life: talk, honest work, compassion, kindness, and warnings against drunkenness and debauchery. He then says that we are to be filled with God's Spirit (5:18). The Spirit does not influence our spiritual activities only. Paul speaks of relationships in the home. He encourages fairness between slaves and masters and responsible living in all our relationships.

The Book of Romans reveals an interesting twist: "This is also why you pay taxes, for the authorities are God's servants, who give their full time to governing" (13:6). Paying our taxes is an act of spirituality.

In his book *Unsplitting Your Christian Life* Michael Griffiths raises a noteworthy point concerning the affirmation given by God at the baptism of Christ. God said, "You are my Son, whom I love; with you I am well pleased" (Luke 3:22). God made this statement to a young man who had spent his whole life in a small village. The man had been working as a carpenter and living at home with His family. We are told little about those hidden years, but so much is suggested in one sentence: "Jesus grew in wisdom and stature, and in favor with God and men" (Luke 2:52). The point: God affirmed Christ in His humanity, and ministry followed.

Christ's humanity was the central issue Satan attacked in the wilderness temptations. Jesus was challenged to prove His humanity by proving Himself spiritually. The challenge was repeated by the crowds at the foot of the cross: "Let him save himself if he is the Christ of God" (Luke 23:35). After all, "spiritual" people shouldn't bleed, suffer, or hurt.

Many Evangelicals who fight for the doctrine of creation often deny it by compartmentalizing life into that which is spiritual and that which is secular. At this point they slip across the border and into the heresy of many cults. Michael Griffiths elaborates on some of the effects of this way of thinking: "It is because of this kind of 'compartmentalization' that Hosea rebukes Ephraim. . . . Israel had plenty of religion, plenty of sacrifices and burnt offerings; but the Lord values mercy towards men and knowledge of Himself more highly than those."[10] The Hebrews of Hosea's day had problems applying spirituality to all of life (see Hos. 6:6; 7:8). Griffiths goes on,

> If we adopt this division of life into sacred and secular, then it must follow that the more time we spend on "spiritual things," the more holy we shall be. Is it not true that for some reason we tend to regard the vocation of the Christian minister or overseas missionary as being a cut above that of the ordinary run of believers? We instinctively feel, no doubt, that he can spend more time saying his prayers and reading his Bible. The common expression "He's in full-time Christian work" simply reeks of the idea that the work of some Christians is intrinsically more Christian than that of others. . . . All Christians, whatever their employment, are full-time Christian workers. If we do not maintain this, we shall be in danger of having a caste system within the Church, a ruling hierarchy who lord it over their humbler brethren.[11]

TOWARD A SPIRITUAL VOCATION

Do you ever feel like a second-class Christian? No one needs to. Through Paul, God affirms all vocations as "spiritual" work. "Brothers, each man, as responsible to God, should remain in the situation God called him to" (1 Cor. 7:24). The surrounding verses make it clear that Paul is referring to situations such as marriage, national and racial customs, and various professions. All roles are ordained and affirmed as called in Christ.

When we compartmentalize life, we step frighteningly close to the world of the cults. God calls us to live every moment creatively before Jesus Christ and under His lordship.

Some might say, "But doesn't Paul elsewhere say we are to place our minds on higher things, to set our 'hearts on things above'?"

Yes, but Paul's statement, as in Colossians 3:1, is not a call to deny reality; it is placed within the context of God's grace revealed in Jesus Christ. Because Christ is now with God, we must focus our minds on Christ. He will free us from guilt so that we can live each day fully and to the glory of God. This is the foundation of self-acceptance, self-esteem, and service to others. Immediately after issuing the call to place our minds on higher things, Paul says, "Whatever you do, whether in word or deed, do it all in the name of the Lord Jesus, giving thanks to God the Father through him" (Col. 3:17).

Paul then fleshes out the implications of this mind-set and this motive for action. He encourages fathers not to embitter children, lest they become discouraged. He encourages slaves to obey their masters. Why? To gain spiritual "brownie points"? No. Because life should be a service to God. Life itself is full-time Christian work. Later in the same chapter of Colossians (just in case his readers misunderstood), Paul repeats himself, saying, "Whatever you do, work at it with all your heart working for the Lord, not for men" (3:23). Yes, the "whatevers" refer to prayer, Bible study, worship, witnessing, and helping the poor, but they also include every other aspect of our humanity.

Scripture begins with creation and climaxes with Christ redeeming all of life (Rom. 8:22–23). The Bible, from the Creation to the final redemption, portrays life as a unity. We are called to be integrated, healthy people devoted to serving God, believers living every minute—with our families, at work, in prayer, and even paying taxes—before God. All facets of life are integral parts of God's will on this earth.

God does lead. God does call people. God does open and close doors. God does direct people to work full-time in missionary work and on the church staff. But God is not limited to working only in the spheres of life that we spiritualize. When we divide life into snug "spiritual" and "nonspiritual" compartments, we are thinking heretically and may blindly accept a cultic view of life. Without our realizing where we are heading, we may walk or cause our children to walk down a road of "spiritualizing" things to validate what God has already ordained as good. Or, on the other hand, we may be in danger of using God's name in vain to justify our irresponsibility, manipulation of others, and spiritual pride. Categorizing time and actions will not only create guilt, but also make us vulnerable to cult leaders who speak our own spiritual language, who are deceptive, who can spiritually move us to a wrong commitment.

QUESTIONS FOR DISCUSSION

1. Can you describe a time when you used the phrase "the Lord led me" to justify a decision? What observations do you have about that?
2. In light of this chapter, does John 3:16 take on new meaning? If so, why?
3. Discuss some instances when God definitely led you or closed doors to you.
4. What questions has this chapter raised for you, and what questions has it answered?

Chapter 4

They Even Share
Their Burdens
and Pray Together

Both Christians and cult members place high spiritual value on group sharing. In both circles, the foundation for community life and growth is the discussion of personal sins, problems, and intimacies. Christians emphasize prayer for each other's problems, but many do not know the hazards involved.

I have met Christians who, during the high emotional pitch of a church or group prayer meeting, have shared intimate details of their lives—and for years afterward have regretted the tormenting results of their admission. A fine line exists between healthy openness and destructive manipulation.

Consider the following questions:

—Do any scriptural limitations protect us from the liabilities of sharing our problems with others?

—Is burden sharing a true sign of spiritual maturity?

—Since both Christians and cult members place value on group prayer for problems, how do we protect ourselves from stepping over the line that separates us?

—Are there innate dangers in sharing intimacies?

—How much should we tell, and to whom should we tell it?

—Does God ask that everything be told?

—Does a church, fellowship group, friend, or pastor have the right to pressure us into sharing intimate secrets?

—What *are* the biblical guidelines?

When sharing problems, difficulties, and burdens becomes a sign of spirituality, the door to manipulation, exploitation, and other unhealthy group dynamics is unlatched.

Might we elevate one truth of Scripture and give it much higher value than does Scripture? During the seventies I visited a church in California that centered around sharing and praying for personal problems—an emphasis with which I concur. But I quickly noticed that the emphasis in this congregation left little room for victories or for ordinary good days. Such a premium was set on "struggling" that one felt spiritually inferior if he or she wasn't always routing sin. My friendships with people in this congregation became difficult as I always felt the pressure to share bearing down on every conversation. We couldn't go out to eat, attend a concert, or go to the beach without spending some wrenching time sharing our struggles.

When pushed to its limit, this subtle pressure to share our struggles can lead to sessions in which people are forced to "confess" wrongs they never committed or thoughts that never entered their minds. In some groups it's not acceptable to "pass" when you feel no particular trouble haunting you.

The following three accounts tell of various group-sharing sessions. The first is from the Congressional Record of May 15, 1981, and it describes Jonestown; the other two are from an article on an Evangelical fellowship based in New England, published in *Boston* magazine.

> As a complement to the physical pressures, he [Jim Jones] exerted mental pressures on his followers. . . . [Tactics included] so-called "struggle meetings" or catharsis sessions in which recalcitrant members were interrogated, required to confess their "wrong-doing," and then punished with alternate harshness and leniency.[1]

> "Community adults would decide what my sin was, then just lay into me," she recalled. "I wasn't allowed to speak to my father when he phoned; they told me it was the Lord's will that I not speak with him. . . . The way I was making beds looked 'rebellious' to them, so I was assigned to scrub the bathrooms. Each day I'd get yelled at and forced to scrub them again."[2]

> "They pushed me into saying I lusted after my little daughter," said Brad Mason (not his real name). "Their idea was that only when you recognize your total depravity can you let Jesus go to work."[3]

In this decade of religious and spiritual confusion, it is important to examine biblical attitudes and guidelines for discussing intimacies, problems, and secret sins with pastors, fellowship groups, and prayer groups.

Exploitation and manipulation in this regard can be very subtle and spiritual sounding. One short conversation with a minister opened my eyes to this deception. I was having an excellent day—one of the best in several months. My minister friend asked, "How is it going?"

"Fine," I responded.

But that wasn't what he wanted to hear. He placed his hand on my shoulder and asked, "How is it really going?"

Suddenly I felt guilty, as though something were wrong with having a good day. A little later he commented, "Your cold is getting to you, isn't it?" It really wasn't, but I began to wonder what I was projecting.

The misuse and exploitation of basic counseling skills, which should be reserved for formal counseling sessions, can place others in a vulnerable position. It can make them dependent on our support, concern, and spiritual parenting. Many pastors and leaders are experts at playing this game of one-upmanship. It can be a subtle tool that forces others to pay homage to our insights and our concerns for them. Many people assume that leaders or other Christians know more about them than they do about themselves. When this assumption is encouraged through the subtle misuse of counseling skills, we are fair game for exploitation.

Christ modeled for us the importance of selectively discussing and revealing personal struggles. Did you ever wonder how disciples like Matthew knew about the temptations of Jesus Christ? Christ obviously told His close friends about these deep struggles and difficulties.

Scripture calls us to confess our faults, sins, and problems to God and to each other. Yet all the guidelines of Scripture warn us to remember that, in all relationships, we are the guardians of each other's vulnerabilities. This is spelled out clearly and practically.

COMING OUT OF THE CLOSET

The seventies may go down in history as the decade when everyone "came out of the closet." Our society and culture encourage people to "let it all hang out," to "tell all." Is this also the call for the believer?

Christ had something to say about "coming out of the closet" when He taught the disciples about prayer: "When you pray, go into your room ["closet," KJV], close the door and pray to your Father, who is unseen. Then your Father, who sees what is done in secret, will reward you" (Matt. 6:6).

Following this instruction, Jesus taught them how to pray publicly. He emphatically pointed out that not everything should be taken out of the closet. Jesus Christ protects our privacy.

Cults and some encounter groups are not the only parties guilty of negating privacy; some Evangelicals pressure people under the guise of spirituality. Such disregard for privacy is the spirit of our decade. This exploitation is the infection of our age.

Christ's words are the antibiotic that will fight against the infection of personal exploitation.

Paul reiterates Christ's position. Although he tells us to speak the truth in love (Eph. 4:15), he doesn't encourage us to tell everything. Speaking the truth in love does not mean having a cathartic session. Paul himself didn't spill all. To Timothy he wrote, "Here is a trustworthy saying that deserves full acceptance: Christ Jesus came into the world to save sinners—of whom I am the worst" (1 Tim. 1:15).

When referring to his sin, Paul used the present tense, saying he was currently in need of God's grace. Note that Paul never told what his secret sins were, the nature of them, or his weaknesses. He spoke truthfully, but he didn't list all the details. Paul guarded his own vulnerability. This basic principle will also protect us from those who might seek to exploit our frailties. Secret sins are to be dealt with secretly. We have the freedom and are encouraged to keep some confessions between ourselves and God. It is important for us to respect others' decisions not to discuss personal inner struggles. Christ discussed His own temptations of His own free will.

WHO HEARS WHAT?

Scripture not only protects our personal privacy, but protects interpersonal problems from becoming tools of exploitation. Sins against another person are to be addressed only with that person and with careful consideration for that person's vulnerabilities. If the issues cannot be resolved personally, then and only then should the problem be brought before mediators.

> "If your brother sins against you, go and show him his fault, just between the two of you. If he listens to you, you have won your brother over. But if he will not listen, take one or two others along, so that 'every matter may be established by the testimony of two or three witnesses.' If he refuses to listen to them, tell it to the church; and if he refuses to listen even to the church, treat him as you would a pagan or a tax collector" (Matt. 18:15–17).

This passage leads us to protect relationships, seek reconciliation, maintain respect, and guard each other's weaknesses. When we are wronged by someone, God calls us to contact that person individually, not the congregation or another friend. He asks us to walk down a private road, not a public thoroughfare. He asks us to fight our own battles, not to drag others in to join our defense or our offense. Again, privacy seems to be the biblical standard for the handling of problems.

If difficulties arise or sins are committed against a group or community, the scriptural model calls for dealing with the problem in the group. Paul publicly challenged Peter in Antioch when he followed Galatians into legalistic enslavement (see Gal. 2:11 and Acts 15). His example can serve as a guideline for group confrontation and submission.

We must always return to a biblical base to guard us against the potential abuse of "community." Evangelical groups and cults that misuse or exploit the sharing of problems reverse the scriptural order; they emphasize confessing private issues publicly, confessing their neighbor's faults one to another, and secretly taking to God those issues that should be openly confronted.

There's no getting around it: Sin that we do not face will ultimately destroy us. When we are isolated by sin, we are most vulnerable to guilt and exploitation by other people. God has given us practical guidelines for our own benefit and growth. When we discuss others' problems with third parties, we magnify the problems, for we become a part of them. The circle of confidence in our lives should only be as wide as the sin committed. Unless we are willing to facilitate the solution, we become part of the problem.

Learning these basic protective principles will prevent us from doing all the right things in the wrong way. How easy for us to get turned around! It is exactly what happened to Judas Iscariot. After he betrayed Jesus, Judas was sorry for his sins. He confessed them; he was penitent; he even returned the blood money. Sadly, Judas did all the right things in the wrong way. Confession was not enough. He confessed his sins to the high priest and elders rather than to God. As a result he felt no resolution, no release of guilt, and he ultimately destroyed himself. Could it be that many of those who died in Jonestown were doing all the right things—in the wrong way?

KNOWING OURSELVES FIRST

Paul wrote to the church in Ephesus and urged them "to live a life worthy of the calling you have received" (4:1). Then Paul defined the various characteristics of the calling: "Be completely humble and gentle; be patient, bearing with one another in love. Make every effort to keep the unity of the Spirit through the bond of peace" (4:2–3).

Notice the imperative of the last statement: "Make every effort. . . ." In any community, quality relationships do not automatically happen. Because we live in a fallen world, deterioration is the normal process of events. God calls us to be diligent in developing our own character and meaningful, trusting relationships with others. A church's unity of the Spirit is not created through meetings, activities, programs, or pastors. Within this context, unity has been established by God in Christ. We are merely caretakers, called to nourish, guard, protect, and maintain this unity through the bond of peace. Scripture does not picture peace as an absence of conflict, but as confidence in God's sovereign hand in the midst of conflict. The bond of peace is made strong by five qualities, like five strands of rope: *humbleness, gentleness, patience,* and *forbearance* in *love.*

When we are humble of mind, we recognize ourselves for who we are. We realistically face our strengths, weaknesses, and limitations. I make a point of separating limitations from weaknesses. Many Evangelicals and cult members confuse limitations with sin. But limitations are the marks of our humanity. Even before the Fall, man and woman were limited in their abilities and knowledge. They were not—*we* are not—God. Limitations are the marks of the created. Weaknesses, however, are those sins and emotional difficulties that have resulted from living in a fallen and fractured world.

When we become aware of God's grace, patience, and gentleness in dealing with our limitations and weaknesses, we can start being patient with others. Gentleness and patience develop in the context of humbleness of mind. When we are aware of and sensitive toward our own clay feet, we are best able to be sensitive to and guardians of the vulnerabilities of our fellow believers.

SUFFER WITH ONE ANOTHER

The Greek *anechomai,* commonly translated *forbearance,* is used fifteen times in the New Testament. It means "to put up with, to tolerate, to suffer with the weaknesses of each other's personalities." Can God mean that we are to suffer with each other's temperaments, dispositions, and brokenness?

Paul understood that our personalities are always with us. A community maintains the unity given by God's grace when its members tolerate, put up with, and suffer with each other, not when they build expectations of perfection. How can we tolerate and suffer with our fellow believers, when we cannot tolerate our own temperaments? God in His grace points us down a road of humility.

Most of us do not enjoy being hemmed in by the givens of our personalities. We can give ourselves emotional claustrophobia. Because we are created in the image of God, we are brimful of mystery and complexity. On top of that add the many consequences of the Fall, sin, mixed motives, genetic and personality weaknesses, and we are asked to put up with a lot.

Keep in mind that the compulsive person in your church or fellowship may not relish the time he or she spends organizing and reorganizing. The absent-minded person is often embarrassed when he or she walks in late. Not all behavior that appears to be antisocial is passive aggression. When the givens of our personalities surface, we wish we could acquire the best qualities of everyone we know. "Why can't I be like so-and-so? More organized? A better provider? More positive? More successful?" Or, instead of being intolerant of ourselves, we might turn our demand for perfection outward, toward others, and say, "Why can't my pastor be like that pastor? My partner like that person? My children more like the Waltons'?" These high expectations make us vulnerable to cult leaders who promise easy, formula solutions for minimizing the complexities of individual and community life.

MAKING OTHERS IN OUR IMAGE

Paul encourages us to forbear each other in love. In the stage musical *My Fair Lady*, Henry Higgins asks, "Why can't a woman be more like a man? . . . Why can't a woman be like me?" We all have our own preludes and fugues developed on this same theme. We may not, like Higgins, sing the tunes aloud, but how often do we repeat the sentiment in attitude, action, and body language?

Do the following words sound familiar? "I love you so much that I am going to relieve you of the burden of your personality. I am now enlightened, and it is my responsibility to follow God's guidance and create you in my own image." When Christians demand of each other Xerox lifestyles and stifling conformity, they create an environment of unhealthy loyalty that can easily be shifted to a cult. Cults want to create followers into given images set by the group or group leaders. We become vulnerable to this photocopy lifestyle when we confuse compatibility with sameness and unity with uniformity. Forbearance assumes diversity. When the standard is conformity, what is the need for tolerance, for "putting up with" each other, for wearing patience and gentleness?

Paul calls us to be diverse in our relationships and to minister to each other the gospel of peace. Christians are called to help others be at peace with who they are.

LEARN TO SAY NO

Because we live in a fallen world, people—even Christians —may try to manipulate us. In such situations we must know how to say no without feeling guilty. We must look to the Scriptures for guidelines that will help us discern: When should we say no, and when are we required to go the second mile?

Many burdens and problems presented to us are legitimate, but others are not. God's wisdom in dealing with the burdens of a group far surpasses our own. Paul elaborates on this issue in his letter to the Galatians:

> Carry each other's burdens, and in this way you will fulfill the law of Christ. If anyone thinks he is something when he is nothing, he deceives himself. Each man should test his own actions. Then he can take pride in himself, without comparing himself to somebody else, for each one should carry his own load (6:2–6).

Notice the checks and balances that protect both parties. Each person is responsible for carrying his or her own burdens. We are not to drop ours at someone else's feet and expect that he or she will carry them, *but* we are to carry the burdens of others.

Scripture does not ask us to remove other people's burdens from them. It asks that we bear them. God does not call us to snatch away from others their burdens, because when we carry our own burdens, we grow. If we take away someone's difficulties, we make them overdependent on us. The goal of the Christian life is dependency on God. Any dependency short of that makes us open to deception and manipulation.

In this fallen world we all are subject to the heavy weights of ill health, aging, and unexpected tragedies. We must not feel guilty for sharing exceptional legitimate needs, for bringing our burdens to the attention of other Christians. We should not feel guilty when our circumstances allow others the opportunity to serve, care, grow, and love.

Bringing a burden to others is being willing to confess needs and acknowledge that life has laid on us burdens that we cannot carry alone. Being a burden involves climbing into another person's arms and letting him or her carry both us and the burden.

Paul goes on to place this instruction in the context of encouragement: "Therefore, as we have opportunity, let us do good to all people, especially to those who belong to the family of believers" (6:10). We will not always have our parents, partners, children, or material possessions. Someday all of the gifts of this life will be stripped away. Paul encourages us to serve each other in the midst of forbearance or tolerance.

On occasion, friends or colleagues may call on us to be their lightning rod—to receive and soak up the shock of their burdens. To be effective and not destroyed in the process, a lightning rod must be grounded. When taking this role, we need to be grounded in humbleness of mind, patience, gentleness, prayer, and God's Word. Only then can we absorb the shock in a godly way.

QUESTIONS FOR DISCUSSION

1. How have the categories and guidelines presented in this chapter been helpful?
2. What is your response to the statement "Unless you are willing to be part of the solution, you will become part of the problem"?
3. What is the danger in our spreading someone else's need before a larger group as a prayer request? How can you guard against violating privacy or confidences?
4. Have you ever felt manipulated into sharing personal, private problems? How can you sensitize yourself to the needs of privacy of others?

Chapter 5

But We Have
a New Testament Church

Many cults, as with numerous Evangelical groups, present themselves as being modeled after the New Testament church.

We all long and search for the "ideal" Christian community. We all have high expectations of the model Christian church. As Christians we esteem the New Testament church as our foundation and its fellowship as the goal for our community life. But beware. These expectations can make us unbiblically close to many cults who claim to be "the only true church since Bible times."

Often students boast that their home churches are patterned after the first-century church described in the New Testament. With stars in their eyes they tell me of their congregations' thrilling impact and the evidence of God's blessing upon them. I do not deny their claims, but they frequently forget that the New Testament church was constantly beset with doctrinal, behavioral, even racial problems.

The Corinthians, for example, tolerated sexual aberration, misunderstood the resurrection of the dead, and misused the gifts of the Spirit, and some even got drunk at Communion services. The Galatians misrepresented the gospel and turned to legalism for a time. The church in Colosse mixed Christian teachings with heathen world-views.

Before we boast too loudly of being another New Testament church, we should reread Scripture carefully and comprehensively. The fragile first-century church needed constant apostolic instruction, guidance, confrontation, and direction. Can we expect more from our "New Testament church"? Many cults describe themselves as ideal communities; they promise perfect fellowship. Our yearning and search for such an ideal can quickly turn our heads in the direction of those who offer something beyond what God is committed to establish in the here and now with fallen and redeemed human beings.

Dietrich Bonhoeffer saw this problem creeping into the German church before the establishment of the Third Reich. He wrote,

> God hates visionary dreaming; it makes the dreamer proud and pretentious. The man who fashions a visionary ideal of community demands that it be realized by God, by others, and by himself. He enters the community of Christians with his demands, sets up his own law, and judges the brethren and God Himself accordingly. He stands adamant, a living reproach to all others in the circle of brethren. He acts as if he is the creator of the Christian community, as if his dream binds men together. When things do not go his way, he calls the effort a failure. When his ideal picture is destroyed, he sees the community going to smash. So he becomes, first an accuser of his brethren, then an accuser of God, and finally the despairing accuser of himself.[1]

What do you think of when you envision fellowship? I often hear Christians saying, "There is no real fellowship in my church. I wish we had fellowship like they did in the New Testament church." You have probably heard and perhaps said something like, "I sure wish I belonged to another church, where there is deeper fellowship."

Let's be honest. How often do we think of fellowship in terms of nice people and what they can do to make us feel better, more comfortable, or more fulfilled? Our modern misunderstanding of fellowship is complicated by "me-first" messages presented in the religious media, which picture the church as the cosmic supermarket, a consumerist field day. We come to God with our spiritual credit cards to receive, on demand, all the displayed benefits. This system requires, however, no down payments, no installments, no responsibilities, just an I.D. We give nothing and in return receive warm feelings and participate in innumerable exciting activities. "Let's see. What would I like today? . . ."

What are the biblical definitions of fellowship? You may be surprised to find that fellowship in the New Testament is not equated with human-centered warmth or satisfying activities. Fellowship can never be created by us, only by God.

The apostle John states that true fellowship is found first in an understanding of God's grace.

> That which was from the beginning, which we have heard, which we have seen with our eyes, which we have looked at and our hands have touched—this we proclaim concerning the Word of life. The life appeared; we have seen it and testify to it, and we proclaim to you the eternal life, which was with the Father and has appeared to us. We proclaim to you what we have seen and heard, so that you also may have fellowship with us. And our fellowship is with the Father and with his Son, Jesus Christ. We write this to make our joy complete (1 John 1:1–4).

John points out that Christian fellowship is based on an orthodox understanding of the person and work of Jesus Christ. Out of our knowledge of Christ comes our joy.

I once taught that we break fellowship with God every time we sin. I can remember hearing church conference speakers say that sin hinders fellowship. If that is true, the logical way to maintain fellowship with God and others is to refrain from sin. God hates sin, and I agree that we are to turn our backs on it. But if lack of sin is the criterion for a Christian's fellowship with God and others, what a precarious and dangerous tightrope we walk. We are left with no security. No wonder the cults are growing!

The Bible really gives us a much broader hope.

> This is the message we have heard from him and declare to you: God is light; in him there is no darkness at all. If we claim to have fellowship with him yet walk in the darkness, we lie and do not live by the truth. But if we walk in the light, as he is in the light, we have fellowship with one another, and the blood of Jesus, his Son, purifies us from all sin.
>
> If we claim to be without sin, we deceive ourselves and the truth is not in us. If we confess our sins, he is faithful and just and will forgive us our sins and purify us from all unrighteousness. If we claim we have not

sinned, we make him out to be a liar and his word has no place in our lives (1 John 1:5–10).

The key to fellowship with God is the work of Jesus Christ through which we repent and receive the grace and mercy of God. Fellowship grows as we walk in the light.

John uses some serious words: *deceive; lie; God's word is not in us; we make God a liar.* Consider what he says about walking in darkness as opposed to walking in light. If we live in darkness, we live in deception. If we live in deception, we live in unreality. If we live in unreality, we make God a liar. By contrast, if we live in the light, we are continually cleansed by Christ's blood.

Within this context John says that if we live or act as if we do not have sin, we are walking in darkness—and that is deception. If, on the other hand, we walk in the light, we *have* fellowship with God. If sin kept us from fellowship, then we would never have fellowship!

A friend once admitted to me that he had not sinned in more than three years. He had "found the secret," he claimed. He had resisted all temptation and continually "practiced the presence of God." He obviously didn't consider spiritual pride a sin. John clearly states that when we claim we have no sin, we walk in darkness.

Many cults dangle the sin-free life in front of prospective members, but many Christians mistakenly reach for and expect the same prize.

Now, John says that if we walk in the light, we have fellowship. But if this does not mean living sinlessly, what does it mean?

Merely acknowledging reality. Have you ever walked into the playroom of a five-year-old in pitch darkness? You are taking your life in your hands! However, when you turn the light switch, you see what looks like the aftermath of a tornado. When the light is on, you watch your step; you are careful not to trip; you bend over to start cleaning up the disaster area and put the room in reasonable order. Light exposes reality and displays facts. Light reveals things as they are.

Notice John's use of the action verb *walk*. Walking assumes the ability to move, make decisions, be aware of directions, and initiate choices. If we walk in God's light, we see facts as they are and we choose to deal with them. Light reveals our sin.

DOES SIN HINDER FELLOWSHIP?

As a child I was taught that walking in the light spiritually involved walking in sinless perfection. As long as my life was free from sin, I was walking in the light. In studying Scripture further, I have been forced to challenge this teaching as unbiblical and basically cultic. This view of the Christian walk says that if one thinks about immorality, bitterness, resentment, or exaggeration then suddenly he or she is in darkness: "Oh, now I have to breathe out a confession, so I can return to the light. . . . Wow! I am perfect again. . . . Whoops! Thought a bad thought; now I am out of fellowship again." This kind of thinking easily leads to schizophrenic behavior and deception in our fellowship with God and others.

According to John, walking in the light includes living with our sin and acknowledging our brokenness, vulnerability, and difficulties. Walking in the light enables us to be honest, protects us from spiritual pride, and most important, protects us from those cults that offer a perfect spirituality. Light reveals reality.

Darkness denies or covers up facts. It causes us to trip over the unseen mess in our hearts. Living in darkness will cause us to inflict pain on ourselves and others.

Fellowship is not just having a good time, feeling good, smiling, and sharing spiritual excitement. Fellowship grows when we keep on walking in the light.

Darkness is pretending. Jesus said, "Men loved darkness instead of light because their deeds were evil" (John 3:19). Darkness hides their impure motives, their manipulations, and their transgressions.

John develops his theme by introducing an order of events that runs contrary to much contemporary teaching. He places fellowship between walking and confessing, then he concludes his list with cleansing. Many—myself included—would prefer to change the order so that it reads: walk, confess, be cleansed, and then have fellowship. Such a revised process seems much safer! It would protect us so we could hide our own sinfulness, deal with it in isolation, and then exclaim to anyone who would hear, "Isn't fellowship wonderful!" Walking in darkness, denying reality, allows us the luxury of risking little. But those who risk little gain little. Those who project spiritual perfection, like the Pharisees and some cult members, are shielded from spiritual growth.

Have you ever met a spiritually perfect person? Did you view him or her as living on a higher plane than yourself? Did you assume that person was sinless? If so, you are standing on dangerous ground. In his writings John establishes that God's grace in Christ frees us to *trust* the presence of God; we do not have to discover the spiritual gymnastic program that will allow us to *practice* the presence of God. God is present with us in all circumstances. His light continually illuminates sin, which, if we confess, His grace continually cleanses.

Fellowship is facing sin, obeying God's Word, learning, praying with, growing alongside, and serving others. The whole of life is the arena in which we fellowship together.

The church is called to reveal Jesus Christ to each other and to the world by living together in reality, honesty, and love. We are not called to witness to spiritual perfection, but to our need for God's daily grace.

With whom did Jesus have the greatest difficulty in this matter? The Pharisees, whom He called "hypocrites" (Matt. 23). The Greeks originated the word to denote an actor, one who played a role. To Jesus, the Pharisees' spiritual life was a colossal theater production.

Jesus Christ cannot give us growth or help us to be obedient if we act out a part—if we walk in darkness.

John was writing to believers, not to unbelievers. When we see and feel guilt over problems, secret sins, and struggles, we should rejoice. God is at work in our lives. The light has been turned on. God loves us and wants to help us clean up the mess.

What is darkness? Boasting of our spiritual maturity and perfection, playing a part that hides our true humanity.

John helps us to see and understand the nature of God's light so we won't spiritually trip up and sin. Note how he continues: "My dear children, I write this to you so that you will not sin" (1 John 2:1).

Quality fellowship begins here. The foundation for healthy Christian fellowship is not attending activities and sharing warm feelings, but walking in light.

WALKING IN LIGHT CAN HURT TOO

Once when I was in upstate New York for a conference, I took my children on a tour of a vineyard. The guide pointed out that every vine is cut back during the coldest weeks of January. If this isn't done, the more productive plants "take over" and smother the others, eventually reducing the quality of the overall crop. Such cut-back plants have long life spans. The ones left unpruned eventually stop producing quality grapes and die prematurely. The guide also noted that until a vine is seven years old, its grapes are not made into wine; only after years of pruning and patience does a crop reach its full sugar potential. During those first seven summers and winters the roots grow deep, becoming less and less vulnerable to root diseases. They intertwine with the root systems of other plants, and together they hold onto the nourishing topsoil.

Jesus reminds us that the Vinekeeper cuts back all the plants. Often Christians take new converts and immediately hold them up as spiritual trophies. Upon conversion, a black activist of the sixties was placed in a position of authority and leadership; he now heads a church that has cultic leanings. Could the Evangelical community have prevented his waywardness if they had allowed God time to make him strong, his roots deep, and his fruit mature?

God is not in a hurry. He deemed Moses ready to lead His people only after eighty years of training. Jesus was thirty when He started His public ministry. Paul spent the first few years of his Christian life in solitude and isolation. If we walk in the light, we will be pruned by the Vinekeeper. Being pruned involves facing sin. If we walk in the light, we will produce quality fruit, which only comes with time and the slow but sure development that accompanies it.

Too often our impatience with God, ourselves, and others gets us into trouble. We want perfection; we want fault-free fellowship; we want the promised utopian community now. But we, along with the rest of creation, groan for our final redemption. We are in the growing stage.

A PART OF THE BODY?

Our confused expectations of fellowship and our insistence on rapid-growth Christianity, coupled with our independent attitudes, contribute to our susceptibility to cults. Many churches have been established in reaction to liberalism or as an offshoot of a church that didn't seem to offer adequate fellowship. In cases where believers from such reactionary churches possess a shallow tradition and lack the authority a time-honored tradition brings, they are extremely vulnerable to the whims of a leader who might move them in a cultic direction.

The countryside is dotted with independent cults as well as "independent" Bible churches, apostolic assemblies, and fellowship groups. If you are part of an independent church, you need to ask some serious questions in light of Scripture. From whom are you independent—from God? from Christ? from the rest of the body of Christ? Can the arm say, "I have no need of the foot"? Are you finding your identity in opposition to another Christian group? Can you be faithful to Scripture and cut yourself off from the rest of the body?

Both independent Christians and cults tend to confuse unity with uniformity. They tend to produce photocopied people. But they are not alone. Many of us stand on old traditions associate only with our own kind—Charismatics with Charismatics, Baptists with Baptists, Presbyterians with Presbyterians, Nazarenes with Nazarenes. We seek out those who will reinforce our own likes and dislikes. How quickly we can grow blind to the rich diversity God has built into the body of Christ! How quickly we can grow blind to our own sin of writing off or discounting other members of the body of Christ! Such blindness brings with it a warm security, an assurance that *we* are *the* body. It allows us to identify ourselves in opposition to, rather than as a part of, a larger group. By remote control it removes from us our responsibility to "love one another" (John 13:35).

All cults view themselves as being independent and identify themselves in opposition to other bodies. When independent attitudes are coupled with a misunderstanding of the believers' walk in the light, Christians are easy prey to a community that eternally promises "something better."

＊Again, Evangelicals are seldom drawn into a cult because they agree with the cult's doctrine. Rather it happens because they see and want signs of great "spirituality." We must always keep before us John's discussion of walking in the light. We are not called to have great faith in God, but to have faith in a great God.

QUESTIONS FOR DISCUSSION
1. How often or to what extent do you define yourself in opposition to others?"
2. If you call yourself an "independent Christian," define yourself in light of 1 Corinthians 12:12–20.
3. Why is it difficult to accept diversity within the body of Christ?
4. Why is it so easy to confuse uniformity with unity? How can a call for uniformity be a form of manipulation?
5. Unbelievers sought out Christ. Do they seek you out? Do you think they feel like people or targets in your presence?

Chapter 6

You Just Have to Hear Our Pastor!

"You just have to hear our pastor!"

Sound familiar? I sometimes get the feeling Christians are more excited about their pastors than about Jesus Christ. Take the time to evelute your expectations of your pastor. Do you expect an eternal flow of new, great wisdom, always presented with a flair? Do you build up unbiblical, superhuman expectations of leadership?

Occasionally I receive job descriptions from churches in search of a pastor. Sometimes their expectations are so absurd, they might as well require that the new pastor take yearly mission trips to Africa—without the aid of a boat or a plane.

Recently a church in the Boston area called a new pastor. On the first Sunday evening he asked each member to write down what he or she considered the eight most important duties of an ideal pastor. He asked them to enumerate next to each item how many hours per week the pastor should give to this activity. Later he added up the largest number of hours expected for each category. The final tally showed that the ideal pastor was expected to spend 22 hours a week visiting; 18 hours studying; 20 hours counseling; 15 hours administering; 15 hours preparing and leading services; 4 hours attending community activities; 10 hours evangelizing, and 2 hours meeting with other local clergy. Total: 106 hours of work per week. Unfortunately they forgot such necessities as rest, sleep, prayer, eating, family relationships, home maintenance, and recreation. Any pastor who fulfills all a church's expectations risks functioning like a cult leader. Both Evangelicals and cult members seem to need and want an authority figure with charisma.

Not long ago two strong Evangelical churches, one in the East and the other in the Southwest, applied for loans that would allow them to build new sanctuaries. The banks granted the loans on condition that the pastor contractually agree to stay for an extended period of time. In both situations the bank felt the congregation was built around and held together by the personality of the senior pastor.

What an indictment of the direction of many Evangelical churches! But this is not an issue unique to local congregations. Almost every major, successful, contemporary parachurch ministry is built around a single personality, who is able to attract a coterie of dedicated followers.

These followers tend to place on their leaders unbelievable pressure to perform. Such pressure opens the door to misuse of power, unhealthy dependency, and discouragement. In her excellent book *They Cry, Too!*, Lucille Lavender points out how our expectations can create overwhelming grief and pain to those who minister.[1] In self-protection a leader can easily give in to the unrealistic and unbiblical demands placed upon him or her. These expectations can force pastors to play roles that run counter to biblical priorities. Unfortunately these roles are also played by cult leaders: Cults offer the ideal pastors who lead the ideal communities.

A certain visitor to the Gordon campus delivered a chapel sermon that was profound, biblical, and challenging, but his style was slow, deliberate, and low-key. Many students who had been raised in strongly Evangelical churches complained that the message lacked spiritual vitality. These students immediately rejected the solid content because it didn't sound "anointed" or "Spirit-led."

Several weeks later another speaker visited campus. His

message contained little Scripture; a majority of the message criticized Evangelicals, social activists, the middle class, suburban life, Western culture, and various Christian organizations. Little in the sermon was biblically instructive or helpful in preparing the students for service, ministry, or growth. The sermon was punctuated with emotionally moving stories. At the end of the presentation, the speaker was given a standing ovation.

Sometime later I asked the same students who had thought the first speaker "unspiritual" what they thought of the second. There was little disagreement: He was definitely a man of God. It was apparent that none could remember the content of his talk, but they all *felt* he must have been led by God. "I felt God's holy presence, and I was challenged to commitment," one student said typically. For the first time I saw and understood how vulnerable Evangelicals are in the presence of forceful leaders—leaders who communicate with a flair.

This is just a minor example of the dynamics present in many churches. The problem is as old as the Scriptures themselves, where Paul defends his own presentation to the Corinthian church.

> When I came to you, brothers, I did not come with eloquence or superior wisdom as I proclaimed to you the testimony about God. For I resolved to know nothing while I was with you except Jesus Christ and him crucified. I came to you in weakness and fear, and with much trembling. My message and my preaching were not with wise and persuasive words, but with a demonstration of the Spirit's power, so that your faith might not rest on men's wisdom, but on God's power (1 Cor. 2:1–5).

Many Christians evaluate pastors, evangelists, and teachers on their leadership, strength, persuasive words, and moving presentation. Perhaps we are frighteningly similar to the parents of Hamelin who invited the Pied Piper to relieve the suffering caused by the rats. We build programs, services, Bible studies, and conferences around personalities whose words will be irresistible, yet we wonder why our people foolishly follow various "pied pipers" to spiritual "never-never lands."

Our attitudes toward a speaker can make us resemble a cult more than we like to think. Most cult leaders exude charisma, personality, and class. They are able to make a follower feel "the presence of God."

To complicate matters, Christian media—both print and broadcasting—often present only success stories, only leaders with overwhelming drive and ability. We must remember that these media of communication have a catalyst in common: marketing.

Scripture was not written with Madison Avenue-type marketing in mind. It records the weaknesses and struggles of God's leaders.

After watching "The Six Million Dollar Man" on television with my ten-year-old daughter, we discussed what a "bionic man" is. As we were talking I turned the TV dial to a station broadcasting an electronic parachurch program. We both listened as the pastor told of his miraculous delivery from a tragic accident. Other passengers lay suffering with pain, even dying. But he just raised his hands, praised God, and climbed out without receiving even a scratch—because of his faith. My daughter looked me straight in the eye and exclaimed, "Wow! They even have bionic pastors."

"Yes," I replied, "but remember, bionic people are half machine."

Jesus bled when He was hurt. He calls us to suffer for and with our fellow Christians.

The mud and mortar of the foundations of all the groups mentioned in the first chapter of this book were made of the perfect church (usually independent) and a powerful leader who, because there was no system of checks and balances, was finally placed in a position beyond confrontation. Most cults allow one or more leaders to confront the laity and call them to accountability, but never the reverse. Ultimately this dynamic results in followers giving over to leaders the complete control of their minds and lives. In many cases leaders are granted more authority over personal matters than Scripture allows.

In an interview with the *Wittenburg Door*, Ronald Enroth, sociologist at Westmont College, stated:

The students I see in religious colleges have come through a long string of leaders. I am not saying these leaders have been bad, but the kids have come to expect leaders to provide packaged Christian answers for them. So they come to a religious college expecting to write down everything the "Christian" professor says *without question*. I do not think we have encouraged Christian young people to think for themselves and we need to teach young people to think critically. We need to encourage young people to make decisions on their own. We need to help the young person develop a personal autonomy (italics added).[2]

Enroth has hit the nail squarely on the head. But adults as well as young students are guilty of looking to the right seminar, teacher, pastor, shepherd, or workshop for instant answers to the complex questions of life.

At a national college chaplains' conference I attended not long ago, all the participants concurred that more and more students are asking the chaplains to make crucial decisions for them. Students want a replacement for their absent pastor or other guru.

This kind of student usually comes from a congregation that has been built around a powerful pastor or leader. This phenomenon in the church is nothing new. Groups have often centered around a spiritual authority who has furthered his or her personal goals. Leaders of such groups often are impelled by genuine beliefs in their ideas, insights, discoveries, and spirituality as being the solutions and answers to the complex problems and ills of society. If the group believes that members can become sinless, the leader, of necessity, must be blind to the fault of his or her own impure motives in dominating and wielding power over others, otherwise their whole foundation falls. If the leader isn't sinless, what is the hope for the laity? This blindness and subtle manipulation and control is not limited to extreme cults like the People's Temple and the Unification Church. Blind abuse of power is also evident in many Evangelical circles.

Ronald Enroth offers a clue as to how and why this can be:

The popularity of evangelical gurus, new-age cults, and superpastors says a number of things about our society as well as rank-and-file evangelicalism. First, there are many people in our rapidly changing and often confusing world who have real dependency needs. They are attracted to authoritarian movements, Christian or otherwise, because these movements offer black and white, clear-cut answers (or systematized approaches) to life's problems. Moreover, the leaders of such organizations convey a sense of solidity, a feeling of being on top of problems, of being in control of the situation. In a word, these groups offer security. For people who have lacked positive structure in their lives, who have difficulty making decisions or resolving conflicts or who are just plain uncertain about the future, these movements/churches/programs are a haven.[3]

If leaders teach submission, obedience, and a strong chain of command without understanding or admitting their own motives, they may become pied pipers leading needy people to a never-never land.

I'M NOT RESPONSIBLE!

Recently I spoke to a woman in deep emotional and spiritual distress. Her problem? She could no longer function, make decisions, pray, and reach out to others because her spiritual shepherd, who for three years had told her what she could and could not do, had moved out of town. She was no cult member; she was active in a prominent Evangelical church in the Boston area.

My first response to her was: "I understand the Bible to say 'The LORD is my shepherd.' Perhaps you have allowed your mortal pastor to take Christ's place."

I personally agree with those who see the benefits of counseling. But I see a danger in asking a counselor, pastor, or friend to be responsible for making personal decisions. This is another old problem—as old as the story of Adam and Eve, who blamed each other for their predicament.

On Judgment Day we will be called to give an account of our own lives. I will have to take responsibility for my own choices and decisions. The same will be true for you. We will not be able to weasel out by saying, "Lord, don't judge me. Judge my shepherd."

Many shepherds and disciples provide not only counsel, but control. They often use God's name in vain by saying, "I have a direct word from the Lord concerning you." Again notice what Enroth has to say on this matter:

When a "delegated authority" provides counsel to those under him, he speaks with God's authority. As Derek Prince, a leader in the discipleship movement, puts it: "Whenever his (God's) delegated authority touches our lives, he requires us to acknowledge and submit to it, just as we would to him in person." Or, as John Robert Stevens of "The Walk" describes it, "If the authority over you is submissive to God, then you are to be submissive to him with your very life."[4]

Does this sound similar to Jonestown?

✳Cult members and Evangelicals often have difficulty admitting that their own leaders are broken people, vulnerable to human frailty and sin. I have pastored in several churches; most were Evangelical, but one was a liberal church on a journey toward a deeper biblical commitment. I saw one major cultural difference between the Evangelicals and the liberals. As a rule, the liberals faced issues openly, admitted their wrongs, and sought forgiveness, whereas many Evangelicals tended to justify or spiritualize their behavior or blame the church authorities and structures for the group's shortcomings and sins. Our inability to deal with our weaknesses and sins as a movement and in our leaders makes us extremely vulnerable to exploitation of leadership similar to that of cults.

Many people were disturbed by the tragic events of Jonestown. Questions were asked: How could this happen in a church? What circumstances allowed a person, in the name of religion, to use, exploit, and so blatantly control others? One theme recurred throughout the whole Jonestown story: power without checks and balances. It is so easy to write Jones off as unorthodox, pathological (perhaps insane), or just demonically cruel. But was he really so different from many of us? We may forget that we are equally capable of building up churches and concepts of spirituality that exploit others, that pit friends against friends, and, on a smaller scale, strive to build subtle power kingdoms that include no checks and balances.

POWER!

God entrusts all of us with some form of power. The misuse of that power is probably the most overlooked and common sin in the Evangelical church today.

In his book *The Violence Within,* Paul Tournier addresses this "will to power" that is so evident in religious groups. He says, "They look upon us as experts, God's mouthpieces, the interpreters of his will. . . . We find ourselves thinking that when they follow our advice they are obeying God, and that when they resist us they are really resisting God."[5]

We all have clay feet. We are all vulnerable to being exploited or exploiting. We all need proper checks and balances to keep leadership in a proper perspective. Paul began by placing the total counsel of God over his life. He said, "I have not hesitated to proclaim to you the whole will of God" (Acts 20:27). Many churches and cults have been built around one aspect of Scripture that was deemed supremely important by the founder. Some cults overly emphasize the inerrancy of Scripture, others teach mainly the Second Coming, some hammer away at the importance of healing, and most cults emphasize evangelism and missionary work.

Ben Patterson, a Presbyterian pastor, stated this most clearly in an article in the *Wittenburg Door.*

> Cultic thinking subscribes to the domino theory of Christian doctrine. Topple one and everything else collapses. This introduces yet another kind of error. If every doctrine is as weighty as every other doctrine, i.e., if a doctrine of . . . angels is of the same weight as a doctrine of the deity of Christ, then nothing is weighty. It is like the aphorism, if everyone is the boss then no one is boss. . . .
>
> If every doctrine is equally important, then any doctrine has a claim to be the center around which a group organizes itself. And what is a cult, but something that has organized itself around a false center?[6]

The Word of God, the Bible as a whole, is the proper guide for our discerning whether or not a teacher is "kosher." When a mesmerized audience or congregation are not thinking in a critical manner about what a pastor with great charisma is saying, they can accept without question statements that cannot even be verified by the Bible as absolute truth.

I recently heard a well-known Evangelical pastor make the following statement on a Christian radio station: "God has raised up America for a witness to the world."

Certainly we hope this is true, but the Bible never specifically spells out the role of the United States. When we unquestioningly accept statements such as these as being absolute, we unknowingly take baby steps away from the biblical authority on which we should firmly stand. We make the words of pastors, evangelists, or teachers equal to or greater than the words of Scripture.

We need to keep our teaching as broadly based as Paul, being careful to encompass the full counsel of God. If a church's message is centered around the pastor's special concern for "body life," balancing adjustments need to be made so that worship is taught and practiced. If relational theology is a church's focus, the base should be expanded to include the teaching of historic theology. This helps keep both church members and special-emphasis leaders from exploiting others.

ALL AUTHORITIES ARE VULNERABLE

What does Scripture say about leadership? One thing is quite clear: The leaders of God needed to be confronted. Moses stood under the law of the Ten Commandments. David was confronted by Nathan. Peter followed the Galatians to another gospel sometime after Pentecost and was called to account by Paul.

Steve Larson writes,

> Moses is not singled out in Scripture as one whose response of inferiority in the face of the Lord's mission of leadership leads to a grand unleashing of the Lord's power. A quick survey of the Bible reveals that recognition of weakness, and consequent dependence upon God's strength, looms as the significant factor in the potency of many Biblical leaders:
>
> *Gideon:* "And the LORD turned to him and said, 'Go in this might of yours and deliver Israel from the hand of Midian; do not I send you?' And he said to him, 'Pray, Lord, how can I deliver Israel? Behold, my clan is the weakest in Manasseh, and I am the least in my family.' And the LORD said to him, 'But I will be with you, and you shall smite the Midianites as one man.'" (Judges 6:14–16)
>
> *Saul:* "When Samuel saw Saul, the LORD told him, 'Here is the man of whom I spoke to you! He it is who shall rule over my people.' . . . Saul answered, 'Am I not a Benjaminite, from the least of the tribes of Israel? And is not my family the humblest

of all the families of the tribe of Benjamin? Why then have you spoken to me in this way?'" (1 Samuel 9:17, 21)

David: "And David said to Saul, 'Who am I, and who are my kinsfolk, my father's family in Israel, that I should be son-in-law to the king?' . . . And Saul's servants spoke those words in the ears of David. And David said, 'Does it seem to you a little thing to become the king's son-in-law, seeing that I am a poor man of no repute?'" (1 Samuel 18:18, 23)

John the Baptist: "He must increase, but I must decrease." (John 3:30)

Paul: "And I was with you in *weakness* and in much *fear* and *trembling;* and my speech and my message were not in plausible words of wisdom, but in demonstration of the Spirit and of power, that your faith might not rest in the wisdom of men but in the power of God." (1 Corinthians 2:3–5)

The leaders in Scripture were not only weak at the initial call from God, they were *continuously weak* (Larson's italics).[7]

The power of God given to these leaders was poured into vessels that were permanently weak. These models in Scripture are the opposite of the superstars of cults and of some Christian groups. The antithesis of the misuse of power is gentleness, which is best seen and understood within the framework of strength. Gentle leaders, pastors, or teachers do not force their insights and wisdom on the unlearned, nor flaunt their gifts before those in need. They are patient. They take time for those who are slow to understand. They are compassionate with the weak, and they share with those in need. Being a gentle pastor, shepherd, leader, or teacher is never a sign of being weak, but of possessing power clothed in compassion.

The great mystery of the Incarnation was not the performance of Christ's spectacular miracles; it was His restraint of power over others. Being very God of very God in the form of man, He could at any moment have breathed His enemies off the face of the earth. His meekness is perhaps the greatest manifestation of God's gentleness. Christ possessed divine power over others, yet He refused to use it—even when challenged by Satan and the crowds to prove to them physically that He was the Son of God.

TRUE MARKS OF LEADERSHIP

Quick answers that cut like swords and control like guns are not signs of a speaker's wisdom, but of arrogance, insecurity, and a refusal to face his or her weakness and sin. Because God's purpose is not to control but to encourage, not to tear down but to redeem, His power is always coupled with gentleness, patience, and compassion.

Jesus Christ is to be our model and our only Shepherd. Jesus calls Himself the Good Shepherd (John 10:11). A good shepherd leads, rather than controls, his flock.

Satan tempted Christ to separate ends from means, to prove his victorious leadership by side-stepping the Cross and the pain of relationships, misunderstanding, and time. Christ responded, "For it is written: 'Worship the Lord your God, and serve him only'" (Matt. 4:10). Note that He connects worship and service. Love for God and compassion for others are central in the life of Jesus and should be at the heart of healthy leaders and churches. Any Christian group that does not spark compassion and love for God will lose its direction. Any group that creates arrogant, belligerent people should immediately be suspect.

Jesus is the true model of authority served. In the New Testament, the Greek word *exousia* ("authority") does not imply any jurisdiction over the details of others' lives. Rather, it implies the authority of truth, wisdom, and experience that can be evidenced in a leader who is held up as a special example. Peter encourages Christians to "be shepherds of God's flock that is under your care, . . . not lording it over those entrusted to you, but being examples to the flock" (1 Peter 5:2–3). In Acts 20:30 Paul warns that "even from your own number men will arise and distort the truth in order to draw away disciples after them." Abuse of the discipleship concept began in the first century.

LOOK AT YOURSELF

Leaders who are most gentle, mature, and wise usually are those who are harder on themselves than on their flocks and congregations. Leaders who are not at war against their own humanity and the temptation to control others will soon seek to control and destructively project their own weaknesses onto others. If we are in positions of power over others and we fail to place controls on ourselves, we subtly and unknowingly start to control others. Power that elevates a leader beyond contradiction or check to a bionic position will lead both the leader and the followers down a road marked by broken relationships, exploitation, and control. Power that tempers and checks itself and is wrapped in compassion is the pathway to gentleness, caring, and maturity. Jesus said, "I am the good shepherd. The good shepherd lays down his life for the sheep" (John 10:11). He is our model of service and leadership.

QUESTIONS FOR DISCUSSION

1. Do you think your expectations of leaders are bionic or scriptural? How and why?
2. Have you been exploited by a leader in the past? What were the causes? How did your attitudes or actions contribute to the unhealthy relationship?
3. Do you find you get more excited about the testimonials presented in books and on religious television than the stories in the Bible? If so, why? If not, why is this true for some people?
4. Who are the spiritual leaders in your life? Do you accept everything they say, or do you study, reflect, question, and examine them in light of God's Word?

Chapter 7

But Mormons Don't Drink or Smoke

Terry was an active leader in the youth group of the first church I served in California. He had become a Christian the previous year and gave a glowing testimony.

Then, astonishingly, Terry became a Mormon; he joined the Church of Jesus Christ of Latter-day Saints. My education and inexperience had left me ill-prepared to meet a crisis like Terry's. I still remember my confusion and dumfounded reaction to his defense: "But Mormons don't drink or smoke."

As with many of us, Terry's conversion to Christianity included adoption of specific cultural taboos important to American Evangelicals. These taboos, along with the popular emphasis on personal happiness and group support, confused Terry in his journey toward spiritual maturity. Terry isn't alone in his misguided journey.

Why do many Christians confuse the issues? It could be because we fail to give adequate instruction about the reasons for the convictions. We succeed in giving only inadequate teaching about spirituality. To Terry, those in the enemy camp of the cults showed more consistency in keeping these convictions, deeper group commitment, and more genuine happiness and sincerity. Terry logically concluded, "They must be more Christian."

Evangelicals tend to yoke their definitions of spirituality

with certain cultural convictions. For many, these "don'ts," ignored or barely mentioned in Scripture, become more important than moral issues and commandments clearly presented in God's Word. An overemphasis on taboos has misled some believers to feel more guilty about sipping a glass of wine than about sleeping with a boyfriend or girlfriend.

Five years ago a young student from a well-known Evangelical church sat in my office and tried to persuade me that the affair she was having with a married man was "directed of the Lord." After all, through their love for each other he had accepted Jesus Christ as his personal Savior. Something about our conversation seemed especially absurd, since just six months earlier she had told me of her disgust for Christians who attend theaters and dances.

This kind of lost perspective has made many Christians vulnerable to cults, because most cults hold to "Evangelical" convictions and offer familiar—but more rigid or intense—control and group commitment. In the documentary movie *Deceived,* Mel White interviewed former People's Temple members who told how the congregation en masse was disciplined because one of their members had drunk a glass of wine. This striking similarity between cultists and Evangelicals plays a major part in shifting one's loyalty to a cult. It is a major area of vulnerability for individuals and the church.

Our young people are not the only ones guilty of setting cultural convictions ahead of moral issues. An Evangelical author recently appeared on a popular Christian television program. At the time of the filming this man was separated from his wife and living in adultery (a fact known to many for several years). The most bizarre part of the whole event was the discussion following the interview. The master of ceremonies on the program was having special prayer, asking God to deliver smokers from their habit. The Bible does command that we take proper care of our bodies, and concern for such is to be commended. But focusing on cigarette smoking without squarely facing biblical "thou shalt nots" is to misconstrue the Word of God.

Some years ago I attended a youth seminar where questions

were asked about the importance of some of these Evangelical taboos. The seminar director commented that the closer one walks to Christ, the more one will accept these cultural taboos. How tragic that several years later, in the national news media, this same organization had to acknowledge that some of their staff members, over a period of years, had been involved in sexual sin. Did the emphasis on cultural issues blind them to other sins? This is a very painful issue for many of us to face, but it must be addressed. We cannot overlook this confusion between cultural convictions and biblical absolutes, but neither should we irresponsibly overreact and overthrow all taboos.

What has led to this confusion? Is it only a problem of the twentieth century? Not really. Again we are discussing a problem as old as the Bible itself, and it centers around a misunderstanding of the nature of the Law.

LAW AND GRACE

In both the Old and New Testaments, the Law points out our sin and disarms us by revealing our need for grace and absolutes to guide our lives. Christ expressly states He did not come to destroy the Law, but to complete it (Matt. 5:17).

In Romans, Paul states that we are not under law: "For sin shall not be your master, because you are not under law, but under grace" (6:14). At first glance this looks confusing. But note that the word *law* is not preceded by the article *the*. Whenever such an article is missing, the noun *law* speaks of a principle. Paul is saying that God accepts us, not because we keep the Law, but by and because of grace. However, He is not abolishing the absolutes of the Law itself. It is essential here to understand grace. Grace enables us to deal with our sin and live in obedience to God's absolutes. When we view law instead of grace as the principle or means of acceptance, we place ourselves under the pressures of fear and rejection. At this point believers tend to set rules for themselves and in turn deemphasize God's Law. These new selected restrictions, cultural taboos, and cultural convictions or rules become the new signs of spirituality. Over a period of time these can easily be given more importance than God's Word itself, and ultimately they can lead to legalism. Legalism always destroys the unity of the body of Christ that is given by God's grace. It always pits believers against each other. Spiritual hierarchies develop, and fellow Christians are measured and accepted, not by commitment to God's grace and absolutes, but by how well they adhere to selected restrictions.

With the advancement of communications technology and the ease of travel, we have become more aware of how these voluntary restrictions vary from culture to culture. Consciences in one country or area are trained to feel guilty over things that are not at all condemned in other cultures. I am continually amazed by the many Evangelical institutions and churches that require members to sign pledges saying they will not indulge in such-and-such an activity, when that activity is not condemned in the Bible.

How unfortunate that they view Scripture so lowly! Perhaps such a pledge should list lust, greed, bitterness, gossip, fornication, adultery, hate, and other sins of the mind and flesh. After all, what really is worth enumerating or pointing out? Might our children eventually throw out the baby with the bath water—throw out the biblical absolutes—thinking they are no more important than the culturally formed convictions? Or might they join a cult that encourages the pledging to which they have grown accustomed?

RESTRICTIONS VS. LEGALISM

This might sound contradictory, but I feel we need to place more restrictions on our lives. On every side our society bombards us with temptations to sin in thought and deed. Because we live in a relativistic society where biblical absolutes are ignored, we need to place voluntary restrictions on our lives without becoming legalistic.

When does one become legalistic? This serious question should not and cannot be avoided. Legalism was not invented by the Pharisees. It began in the opening chapters of Genesis, when Eve added her own restrictions to God's firm commands.

> "But you must not eat from the tree of the knowledge of good and evil, for when you eat of it you will surely die" (2:17).

> The woman said to the serpent, "We may eat fruit from the trees in the garden, but God did say, 'You must not eat fruit from the tree that is in the middle of the garden, and you must not touch it, or you will die'" (3:2–3).

In Genesis 2, God commanded only that Adam and Eve not eat any of the fruit. Note that by Genesis 3, Eve had decided she couldn't even touch the tree. But God had given no such prohibition; she had added to God's Word and made her own restrictions equal to His.

Voluntary restrictions on our lives are certainly important and often necessary. But whenever Christians or cult members make the same mistake as Eve, trouble starts brewing.

Admittedly, voluntary restrictions are usually the fruit of a sincere desire to do right and to protect oneself. There is nothing wrong with this. When we protect each other from temptation, we also encourage each other. Restrictions become stumbling blocks when they are elevated to a position of equality with the Bible, when they are transferred from ourselves to others, and when they are prefaced with a verbal or strongly implied "God says."

When we let these restrictions become the basis for church membership, signs of spirituality, acceptance or rejection by a fellowship or community, we start controlling the lives of others. We start creating unhealthy dependence on *our* word, rather than on God's Word and judgments. In so doing, we devalue God's Word and we confuse future generations. We may have logical reasons why such-and-such a conviction makes sense, but when the restriction is preached without the rationale and without room for personal conscience, Christians start feeling guilty about breaking taboos and not about breaking God's absolute commandments. When we reach this point, we are strikingly similar to the cults.

WHAT IS THE PATTERN?

The journey to heresy begins with a misunderstanding of God's grace and a lack of trust in His grace that enables us to keep His commandments. When we, rather than God, are responsible for keeping us in His hands, we are constantly filled with fear. We are always afraid we will commit some minor infraction that will cause our damnation. Because we want to guarantee our purity, we place voluntary restrictions on ourselves and then on others, ultimately confusing them with God's Word. Finally we set them equal to God's Word. Eve, some Christian groups, and most cults share the problem of the Pharisees:

> So the Pharisees and teachers of the law asked Jesus, "Why don't your disciples live according to the tradition of the elders instead of eating their food with 'unclean' hands?" (Mark 7:5).

> "You have let go of the commands of God and are holding on to the traditions of men." And he [Jesus] said to them: "You have a fine way of setting aside the commands of God in order to observe your own traditions!" (7:8–9).

Were the disciples accused of breaking the law? No, not at all. They had merely failed to sign the pledge card saying they would wash their hands before each meal. They had broken the voluntary restrictions of the elders, who had elevated such "traditions" until they were signs of maturity, fellowship, and genuine spirituality.

Might this be the reason why Scripture says so little about the physical qualities of Jesus Christ? If Jesus had worn orange robes, we would no doubt have a holy color of dress. (I personally hate orange!)

Once I traveled with a mission team in Europe. We helped churches to establish "halfway houses" and coffee houses in order to reach members of the sixties' drug culture. I carefully observed the various Protestant subcultures: Some German Evangelicals drank beer, but criticized the French for drinking wine; the French drank wine while criticizing the Dutch Evangelicals for smoking; the Dutch criticized both the Germans and the French. On one occasion I spoke to a British Evangelical group who believed that during worship all women must cover their heads in submission. Ironically, that was the heyday of micro-mini skirts. While preaching, I wished I could stop and ask the women to take off their hats and place them over their laps. Their priorities seemed to be misnumbered. Certainly cultural taboos are needed in every age, but they are not to become points of argument or the cause of ridicule or strife. We must all remember that the body of Christ is made up of many members, including people from many cultures.

MORALLY ABSOLUTE, CULTURALLY RELATIVE

Was the problem of taboos unique to Eve and the Pharisees? No, Paul also had to face this major issue as it related to church leaders in various cultures. We must always remember that Scripture is inflexible morally but flexible culturally. Morally the Bible is always absolute; culturally it is relative. Fornication was as wrong in Jerusalem as it was in Corinth, but the eating of pork was a different matter. The Jerusalem Christians abstained, while the Corinthians freely ate it. Local convictions were determined by nationality—whether or not one was Jewish or Gentile.

The best examples of Paul's cultural flexibility are found in Acts and Galatians.

> He came . . . to Lystra, where a disciple named Timothy lived, whose mother was a Jewess and a believer, but whose father was a Greek. . . . Paul wanted to take him [Timothy] along on the journey, so he circumcised him because of the Jews who lived in that area, for they all knew that his father was a Greek (Acts 16:1, 3).

> Yet not even Titus, who was with me, was compelled to to be circumcised, even though he was a Greek. This matter arose because some false brothers had infiltrated our ranks to spy on our freedom we have in Christ Jesus and to make us slaves. We did not give in to them for a moment, so that the truth of the gospel might remain (Gal. 2:3–5).

Paul understood the Jews and their cultural restrictions. Since Timothy was part Jewish, Timothy was circumcised. For the sake of spreading the gospel Paul felt this outward sign of Timothy's Jewish heritage was important. In the Acts account, Paul honors the cultural norms so the Jews would accept Timothy as one of them.

But in Galatians Paul points out that Titus, who is wholly Gentile, needn't be circumcised. Was Paul being fickle? Why the difference? Why did Paul here take a firm stand against something he had insisted on in the case of Timothy?

The answer is simple. The false teachers near Galatia were following the example of Eve and the Pharisees, who made laws of their personal rules. Paul refused to give in to these teachers who were preaching a false spirituality.

Central to all biblical instruction is our responsibility to make right choices. We are free to make any choice, but we are not called to act on our every freedom. On occasion we must place voluntary restrictions on ourselves. Selected restrictions do not make us legalists. We become legalistic only when we begin to define mature Christianity on the basis of these restrictions and when we use them as means for accepting other Christians into our fellowship or excluding them from it.

WEAKER CHRISTIANS?

Liberty in Christ is not to be confused with the liberation movements of our own culture. Scriptural liberty is not an injunction to discover how many freedoms we have and to flaunt them before others. Ours is a liberty to be reconciled with God and others, even with legalists. Ours is a freedom to be open with God, a freedom to be obedient. Flaunting freedoms has nothing to do with liberty or liberation; it is another form of enslavement, perhaps worse than that of the legalists.

A colleague tells of visiting a pastor who just had to show off his wine cellar. His new-found cultural freedom had become a new-found spiritual enslavement. In being proud of his freedom, he was abusing the liberty Christ gives His followers. Part of the freedom we have in Christ involves acting responsibly toward others who may be weaker than we.

We do have responsibility toward others, especially to the weaker Christian. The Christian life is a corporate life. As soon as we say the first word of the Lord's Prayer, we acknowledge that corporate reality. That one word *our* expresses our theology, responsibility, and relationship with others.

The concept of the stumbling block and the weaker Christian has been greatly misused and misunderstood and is often presented as meaning the opposite of Scripture's intent. We need to study the biblical definition of the "weaker Christian" and separate in our minds that phrase from the "older Christian" and his or her desire to control other people. Control is the heart of all cult groups, and it must not be overlooked as sin, even when it is disguised as concern for the weaker Christian.

Paul exhorts us to be concerned about weaker Christians; he does not exhort us to please legalists. Three Pauline passages address this issue and define the "weaker Christian." The first is in Romans.

> Accept him whose faith is weak, without passing judgment on disputable matters. One man's faith allows him to eat everything, but another man, whose faith is weak, eats only vegetables. The man who eats everything must not look down on him who does not, and the man who does not eat everything must not condemn the man who does, for God has accepted him. . . . One man considers one day more sacred than another; another man considers every day alike. Each one should be fully convinced in his own mind. . . . Therefore let us stop passing judgment on one another. Instead, make up your mind not to put any stumbling block or obstacle in your brother's way. . . . It is better not to eat meat or drink wine or to do anything else that will cause your brother to fall. So whatever you believe about these things keep between yourself and God (Rom. 14:1–3, 5, 13, 21–22).

According to this passage, the persons who place restrictions as signs of spirituality on their lives are the weaker Christians.

> We know that an idol is nothing. . . . But not everyone knows this. Some people are still so accustomed to idols that when they eat such food they think of it has having been sacrificed to an idol, and since their conscience is weak, it is defiled. . . . But food does not bring us near to God; we are no worse if we do not eat, and no better if we do. Be careful, however, that the exercise of your freedom does not become a stumbling block to the weak. For if anyone with a weak conscience sees you who have this knowledge, . . . This weak brother, for whom Christ died, is destroyed by your knowledge. . . . Therefore, if what I eat causes my brother to fall into sin, I will never eat meat again, so that I will not cause him to fall (1 Cor. 8:4, 7–11, 13).

Again, the weaker Christian is the one who abstains. In this passage the cultural issue involves the trappings of a past false religion that equated spirituality with eating meat offered to idols. Your eating meat may cause a certain person to believe in a false religion, may drive that weaker believer back to heathen worship. Paul emphasizes concern for the weaker Christian, who doesn't have the same heightened knowledge and clearness of conscience as others who are free of extrabiblical regulations. Stronger Christians place voluntary restrictions on themselves even when they know these have nothing to do with spirituality or church membership.

Later in 1 Corinthians Paul brings up the matter again.

> If some unbeliever invites you to a meal and you want to go, eat whatever is put before you without raising questions of conscience. But if anyone says to you, "This has been offered in sacrifice," then do not eat it . . . for conscience' sake—the other man's conscience, I mean, not yours. For why should my freedom be judged by another's conscience? (1 Cor. 10:27–30).

As you can see, the Word of God sheds a bright light on how and why we regulate our lives.

In the Book of Romans, Paul views as the strong Christians those who know that meat offered to idols has no special cultic power. The gospel has freed them. Such a freed person could go to the temple market, buy the best steak or the cheapest meat, and—even though it had been offered to idols—eat it with enjoyment. Why? Because of a seared conscience? No. Because of his or her knowledge and understanding of freedom in Christ.

What does Paul mean when he speaks of the knowledge of the judgment of God? The freedom of walking in the Spirit? Law can't give such freedom; only grace can assure us that God is not offended when we eat such meat. He does not condemn such cultural actions.

BLIND IN ONE EYE

We all have weak spots in our lives, usually seen by others but not by ourselves. We are all strong Christians in some matters and weak Christians in other areas of our lives. In these Pauline passages we are not invited to engage in activities blindly and compulsively just to prove our liberty.

The weak Christian is not the one who voluntarily abstains, but the abstainer who sees restrictions as the evidence of his or her (or someone else's) spirituality, the one who cannot exercise a freedom because of a misinformed conscience. The weak Christian is the one whose lips haven't touched cough syrup or perhaps vanilla extract (because of their alcoholic content) for fear they would call down the displeasure or wrath of God.

Paul recognizes that we all bring to the church some baggage accumulated in our younger years. Our past brokenness leaves a residue. Some of us may understand the differences between cultural, voluntary restrictions and biblical absolutes, yet we may not be able to enjoy and live in the freedoms God has granted. Our head knowledge may be ahead of our heart knowledge.

On the other hand, some of us who feel we have thrown off all constricting cultural taboos tend to go off the deep end and go out of our way to offend legalists (a sinful desire similar to the exploitation of cults). It is important to note that Scripture does not bind anyone to obey the legalist rules or give in to one's negative feelings about one's liberties.

If a person who has been a Christian for forty years believes it is a sin to go to a movie, you needn't be uptight. But then again, you should not deliberately flaunt your freedom or offend the person by telling them how great *Chariots of Fire* and *Joni* were at the local cinema.

These issues are not easy to address and not easy to resolve personally. Only with prayer, Bible study, honest self-evaluation, and soul-searching of our motives can we move toward freedom and wholeness in Christ.

Many of us would rather ask our pastor, church, or fellowship group to lay down life-long restrictions than to face the responsibility of making our own decisions. But convictions made by proxy never promote personal growth. They only produce immature Christians, create credibility gaps, and make us vulnerable to cults who function in a similar way.

A GREATER RESPONSIBILITY

As we strip away our legalism, discover our new liberties, and voluntarily select restrictions, we are forced to face the bare bones of the greater responsibility for which we will individually be accountable to God: "All men will know that you are my disciples if you love one another" (John 13:35).

We are to affirm the doctrine of creation and redemption to our families and to other believers—including legalists and older Christians who may seek to control us. At one time or another, all of us will have to make crucial ethical decisions. The group, pastor, cult leader, or fellowship group may not be there to say, "Thus saith the Lord." We must be ready to rest in the knowledge of God's Word, which will enable us to choose correctly, and then act on our choices.

> We proclaim him [Christ], admonishing and teaching everyone with all wisdom, so that we may present everyone perfect in Christ (Col. 1:28).

QUESTIONS FOR DISCUSSION

1. Do you find that you react more negatively to those who transgress your voluntary restrictions than to those who are immoral?
2. Do you agree with this chapter? Why or why not?
3. List any similarities you see among Eve, cult members, some Christians, the Pharisees, and you.
4. Do you agree that we can use our liberties as new forms of enslavement? Has this ever happened to you? If so, how and why?

Chapter 8

The Problem of Pain

Every human has needs and desires they long to have filled and met. They want love, some sense of order, a purpose for and definition of life, some security. Some of these needs can only be met by God, but others can and should be filled by fellow humans and institutions.

Many cults, like many Christian groups, meet these personal needs. When answers—no matter whose they are—are dressed up in Bible verses, many of us turn off our discerning and critically thinking minds. We can be lured and deceived. Many false teachers "stand" on the Bible and claim to have a high view of Scripture, but they pick and choose their pet passages.

James W. Sire points out in his book *Scripture Twisting* that the Bible is used by many modern cults, Hindus, and Buddhists. It is the final authority for Christian Scientists and Jehovah's Witnesses. It is quoted by Sun Myung Moon in his book *The Divine Principle*. It is read by Mormons.[1]

Many Christian churches are built around one aspect of Scripture. Such groups are in danger of treating the Bible as the cults do. This problem can result in leaving the church members susceptible to a group that emphasizes the same issue, even with the same biblical arguments. For example, a church that has been established with single-minded emphasis on biblical prophecy may make its members game for cults that center on similar prophetic Scriptures. Or the opposite may happen: Overemphasis on experience may make a person "revel" in a search for a doctrinal foundation. In that search the believer may be attracted to a cult that seems to be stabilized on a doctrinal structure. Or a church that emphasizes doctrine at the exclusion of warmth and devotion may drive a person under great personal stress into a cult that sincerely seeks to meet and minister to human needs.

My experience reveals that people involved in cults or attracted to groups with cultic leanings have been handicapped by an imbalance in past Christian experience and teaching. Perhaps the most evident is the difficulty many Christians have in facing suffering and affliction. We have been extremely guilty of taking sections of Scripture and using them to reinforce only one-half of the biblical answer to the problem.

Charismatic and Holiness groups emphasize healing. In his book *The Disease of the Health and Wealth Gospels*, Gordon Fee says that certain elements of the neocharismatic movement who claim that no sickness is within God's will are in closer agreement with the teachings of Christian Science than with the whole of Scripture.[2]

On the other hand, the Reformed and dispensational groups tend to emphasize the cathartic benefits of pain. They pride themselves in a kind of naturalism and fatalism that sees God working through circumstances as they are rather than His working to change circumstances.

IF YOU ARE NOT HEALED, IT'S YOUR OWN FAULT

I am indebted to the Pentecostal movement, because Pentecostal Christians introduced me to Jesus Christ. Their faithful desire to teach the Scripture, their many answered prayers, their exemplary lives, the quality of their relationships—all made an early impact on my life and convinced me of the reality of the person and work of Jesus Christ. However, over the years I noticed a pattern that continued to bother me, a pattern that made many of their members open to guilt, despair, loss of faith, even to false teachings of cults.

The problem was this: If God healed a person, the evangelist or minister who prayed for the deliverance was acclaimed for having great faith; if God chose not to heal, the person who was being prayed for was accused of lacking faith. Those who weren't healed went away confused, discouraged, and feeling guilty. This discouragement and hurt was a direct result of teaching based on half of what Scripture has to say on the subject. God does answer prayer. He does heal. But His not healing does not mean that He hasn't answered prayer.

We live in a generation that has been stripped of the Real. We have been handed many synthetic substitutes for natural flowers, food, and cloth. Many prefer artificial flower arrangements over the real thing, for although plastic blossoms have little fragrance, they never wither and die. Our food doesn't quickly spoil, and our synthetic clothes are never eaten by moths.

How easy it is for us to transfer our expectations for the unreal to our thinking on spiritual matters: No more trouble! Daily manna from heaven. Dollar bills falling from the sky. No suffering. No problems. This view of the Christian life is lopsided.

On the other hand, some Evangelicals feel that the Christian life is similar to life portrayed in Sartre's *No Exit:* Always the "heavies," doom, gloom, God working mainly through our trials and tribulations.

I am now associated with the Reformed arm of the Evangelical church. Here I see a lot of this opposite, "hard times" Christianity that claims God works—that is, prefers to work—through our afflictions.

God certainly does work through our crises. But when we view only one side of Scripture, we are as guilty as those who say, "God must heal." This position can also lead to despair and fatalism. It can send Christians looking for the green pastures on the other side in hopes that they will find refreshment from their suffering.

How does one stay firmly planted between these two extremes? How does one live to God's glory in an age of anxiety? On what framework can we cultivate the art of living despite the fractured effects of the Fall? How can we be balanced, biblical believers?

THE SOURCES OF AFFLICTION

The Bible offers four basic reasons why we experience difficulties, afflictions, and suffering. First, we live in a world that has been devastated by the Fall. The irrational and unjust muck of sin is passed on sociologically, genetically, and psychologically. The residue causes disorder, unfairness, unreasonableness, and injustice in every realm of reality. Children are born blind, disabled, and malformed. Disease haunts everyone, for we all carry some physical weaknesses; some of us are prone to diabetes, others to psychological disorders, others to cancer. Still others struggle with tendencies toward sexual deviations. Christians and non-Christians alike are influenced by their physiological, psychological, and sociological surroundings and beginnings. At one time or another everyone gets a cold and has a headache. Everyone bleeds when cut. All people, Christian and non-Christian, die physically. Since the Fall, all of life has been tainted by a persistent element of injustice.

Second, the Bible pictures life as influenced by unseen spiritual forces. Satan is a spiritual reality who acts in every age, plays on human minds, disturbs individuals, and influences nature, families, and world leaders. Satan's purpose is to sabotage God's redemptive work in history by infiltrating the world with sin, suffering, alienation, and confusion.

I was fascinated by a Chinese play I saw once in San Francisco. The stage had two levels. On the upper stage, evil and good spirits battled with each other. The actors on the lower stage could not see the war waging above them, but their actions and scripts were obviously influenced by the supernatural forces. What a fitting reflection of reality as presented in the Bible, where the battles of the unseen world are pictured as influencing every one of us.

Third, we have problems because our actions entail consequences. The mystical Eastern parables that tell of a person entering a body of water that doesn't ripple have no relation to reality. Our choices for good or ill do and will influence our future and the future of others. The destructive and chaotic choices of Jim Jones influenced the lives of many people. The irresponsible drunk or drugged person who drives, hits another car, and cripples someone for life has influenced history for ill. The great spiritual reforms sparked by men such as Wesley, Luther, Moody, and Calvin have changed the course of history for good.

We can bring unnecessary suffering to others. Young mothers who take drugs while pregnant and give birth to children with defects influence their family's history. Such ripples in the sea of life are real and very painful. God has created each one of us with such overwhelming significance that our actions cause real ripples that affect children, families, marriages, nations—every aspect of life for genera tions to come.

Last, God brings difficulties into our lives to help develop us, to strengthen us, to spark our growth, and to cultivate our maturity. The psalmist realized this when he said, "It was good for me to be afflicted so that I might learn your decrees" (119:71).

Do you see the complexity of the problem of pain? How utterly impossible for us to know which issue or issues are the reason for our afflictions. All four causes may be at work at the same time. Scripture does not call us to sort out the "why" of someone's pain, but summons us to "weep with those who weep" and "rejoice with those who rejoice" (Rom. 12:15 RSV).

Does God answer prayer? Of course He does. But not always on our terms or according to our definition. Like the picture drawn in the Chinese theater, the world is larger than one field of vision. Most of the time we are unable to sort through the causes of our situation. This is why we need to study God's Word, pray, and seek counsel from fellow Christians.

Jesus said, "In this world you will have trouble" (John 16:33). How easy it is for us to reflect the thinking of our

society and expect all things to be resolved. Utopian expectations are the core of Nazism, Marxism, and all such "isms"
that lead to dehumanization under the pretext of bringing
happiness for all. Utopian expectations were the core of Jim
Jones's Jonestown community.

Romans 8:28 says, "All things work together for good"
(KJV). Note that Paul doesn't say that all things *are* good. We
are not called to label everything that happens "good." Paul
states a few verses later that nothing in this life can separate us
from God's love found in Christ Jesus—neither crisis, present
history, future events, unseen forces, life, nor death. For the
believer, life, spiritual forces, and death are part of a larger,
good plan. Paul does not say that God's love takes away
difficulties, but rather that it is with us when we are forced to
rub against these raw edges of reality.

PUZZLED SAINTS

Life has always been a complex puzzle. Even for God's
leaders, solutions have never come easily. For their spiritual
survival, believers have had to study, pray, exhibit compassion, and evaluate their own actions and motives.

The mysteries of life, the "whys," have always confounded
great leaders of God. In the Old Testament, Habakkuk sets
forth a complaint against God: "Your eyes are too pure to look
on evil; you cannot tolerate wrong. . . . Why are you silent
while the wicked swallow up those more righteous than themselves?" (1:13). Habakkuk doesn't understand why God's
people go through difficulties.

If becoming a believer meant only receiving the promise of
earthly goodies, wouldn't the whole world believe? Such mis-
representation of the gospel is more than unbiblical; it is
naïve. To claim such is similar to someone saying that sin is
not fun. If sin weren't so pleasurable, why would anyone be
sinning? Why would resisting temptation be so difficult?

Jeremiah—God's chosen prophet, leader of God's people,
and spiritual model—found his mind grappling with these
same puzzling questions: "You are always righteous, O LORD,
when I bring a case before you. Yet I would speak with you

about your justice: Why does the way of the wicked prosper? Why do all the faithless live at ease?" (12:1).

Do you ever ask why the wicked prosper? Jeremiah saw the gospel of "health and wealth and prosperity" as being tied to wicked and scheming people. In essence he was saying, "God, I am having difficulty with Your judgments. I just do not understand." How easy to disregard these questions and statements. But they are a part of God's Word—revelation given for our understanding. God did not condemn Jeremiah or Habakkuk for asking these probing questions, nor did He call into question their faith.

ANSWERS WITHOUT COMPASSION

During a Bible study on the Book of Job, I heard a teacher comment, "The friends of Job misunderstood the causes of his affliction and laid guilt trips on him. We need to see what was going on from the divine perspective—that unseen forces were influencing the seen world. Job should have been able to see his situation in this light."

Although the theology was right, this teacher lacked a deep sensitivity to Job's confusion, difficulties, and hurts. Job didn't have the story of his life down on paper to read. Job didn't understand the "why" of all that was happening. In similar manner we do not always know which forces are at work and why. The important question is, How can God be glorified in this event?

Job couldn't pick up the book named after him and evaluate his own situation as being "just a spiritual battle." No, Job had the same need for compassion, understanding, and spiritual support that we do. He did not need to hear presumptuous assumptions. Simplistic or one-sided spiritual answers did not help Job, and they don't give us much help.

Cult members and some Christians fall into the trap of assuming that they know all the causes of a particular affliction. But in this life we cannot know for sure. In this life we only "know in part" (1 Cor. 13:12). Assuming that we know the cause of a sorrow can be a way of avoiding our difficult responsibility to cry with those who are crying.

How often do we assume we know the cause of other people's difficulties? Can you imagine Job's accusers saying, "You haven't been walking in the spirit"? Or "How is your spiritual breathing?" Or "Obviously your children haven't followed the right chain of command."

What was God's attitude toward Job? God lays it out in the first verse of the first chapter of Job's story: "In the land of Uz there lived a man whose name was Job. This man was blameless and upright; he feared God and shunned evil."

One friend of Job assumed the "obvious": If God were justly taking Job to task, Job would be suffering even more. God was obviously purging him, and even so, God had obviously overlooked some of his sins (see 11:1–6).

It seems another friend, agreeing with the first, had been schooled in basic confrontation counseling techniques and therapy. His "session" was similar to many in cults and questionable Christian groups, where someone's guilt is assumed. Job's friend said, "Your sin prompts your mouth; you adopt the tongue of the crafty. Your own mouth condemns you, not mine; your own lips testify against you" (15:5–6).

To paraphrase, he was urging Job to admit his sin: "You are an evil man. Confess your sins; tell me and the group about them. You lack faith. If you had faith, you would possess health and wealth."

But remember, God thought otherwise: "In the land of Uz there lived a man whose name was Job. *This man was blameless and upright;* he feared God and shunned evil."

I AM CONFUSED: I DO NOT UNDERSTAND

Job kept saying, "I do not understand or see the causes of these disasters." Job knew his accusers were wrong, yet they seemed blind to any conclusions other than their own presumptions. They could not hear Job's cries: "Look at me! Look at me! Can't you see the boils on my face? Here I am. My children are dead. Why? Why do other people's children live on?"

Why do the wicked live on, growing old and increasing in power? They see their children established around them, their offspring before their eyes. Their homes are safe and free from fear; the rod of God is not upon them (21:7–9).

Job had no answers. Yet, always wanting to see God glorified, he cast himself upon the sovereign God: "Though he slay me, yet will I hope in him" (13:15).

The Psalms are filled with similar questions. The psalmists understood the importance of acknowledging to God their confusion. They didn't stop there; they usually went on to proclaim God's sovereignty. The acknowledgment coupled with worship was the beginning of the healing of their perspective. The writer of Psalm 73 spills out his frustrations as he struggles with his loss of perspective, but ends in a doxology.

> When I tried to understand all this [the injustices of life], it was oppressive to me till I entered the sanctuary of God; then I understood their final destiny (Ps. 73:16–17).

Comforters who speak in platitudes and give simplistic answers avoid their responsibility to care, to minister, to be moved with compassion as modeled in Jesus Christ. The root of this avoidance is often related to our inability to deal with our own mortality. We are all terminal. Suffering people remind us that our own lives are fragile. The psalmists, Jeremiah, and Habakkuk knew this. They weren't afraid to be honest with God or ashamed of it. If God hasn't answered our prayer in the way we think He should have, God has still answered our prayer.

Our spiritual battle is no different from any other. It leaves behind wounded and disabled who will heal only if they are nurtured and cared for. When we fail to express compassion and concern to suffering people we come close to being guilty of shooting our wounded. Insensitivity, lack of compassion, and pat answers only deepen wounds. Such responses only make the wounded seek help elsewhere, possibly in some cult or other offbeat group that promises to meet these personal needs.

We all need to learn the art of listening. As God allowed Job and the prophets freely to express their anxieties, so should we. One of the best medicines for those in distress is the company of a good listener, someone who cares, prays, and does not immediately judge circumstances. Hasty judgments may cause us to overlook the boils on suffering faces; we are sure the sufferers are missing their quiet time, are failing to walk in the Spirit, have forgotten how to breath spiritually, or have hidden some secret sin. Let us not forget that those who suffer, live in poverty, face anxiety, and carry in their bodies afflictions may be like Job—blameless and upright.

PRAYER AND FAITH

You may ask, "Doesn't James tell us to pray the prayer of faith for the sick?" Yes, but James 5:14 must be seen alongside the rest of Scripture. Jesus Christ encourages us to visit the sick. Speaking of the Last Judgment, Christ said,

> "Then the righteous will answer him, 'Lord, when did we see you hungry and feed you, or thirsty and give you something to drink? When did we see you a stranger and invite you in, or needing clothes and clothe you? When did we see you sick or in prison and go to visit you?'
>
> "The King will reply, 'I tell you the truth, whatever you did for one of the least of these brothers of mine, you did for me'" (Matt. 25:37–40).

Jesus Christ assumes that the sick and hungry will always be with us. He does not challenge us to legislate political change or to declare their lack of faith. He calls us to care for the needy as though they were Jesus Christ Himself.

Paul tells Timothy to take a little wine for his stomach's sake (1 Tim. 5:23). He isn't implying that the water in his town is less than pure, but that Timothy suffers from some unhealed ailment—in fact, "frequent illnesses."

Even after Pentecost, faith did not protect the disciples from suffering. The Book of Hebrews, for example, presents two sides of faith. Chapter 11 says,

> By faith Noah . . . built an ark (v. 7).
> By faith Abraham . . . was enabled to become a father (v. 11).
> By faith Moses' parents hid him (v. 23).
> By faith the people passed through the Red Sea (v. 29).

The writer of Hebrews goes on to describe the many positive, miraculous results of faith. But any reader who stops at verse

31 fails to see the total picture. Notice the following phrases compiled from verses 32–38: "Through faith . . . some faced jeers and flogging. . . . Others were tortured . . . stoned . . . sawed in two . . . put to death by the sword. . . . They went about destitute, persecuted and mistreated."

The saints suffered sorely by, through, because of their faith.

God does not always paint values as we see them. If a person is suffering, it may be through faith. His or her affliction may not be a sign of weak faith, poor prayer habits, or a lack of maturity; it may be exactly the opposite. If God does not answer a prayer for the removal of sickness in the way we think it should be answered, God is still sovereign. God's sovereignty does not depend on our requests. His plan and sight are bigger than ours.

Does God heal? Yes, the Bible says God heals. (He healed Job!) Does God bless believers with success and financial victories? Yes, the Bible says God does. (Job died an old, rich man.) But if a person faces affliction, he or she may be facing it because of, or through, faith.

The Bible encourages us both to visit the sick and to pray "the prayer offered in faith" for the sick. God delivered Peter from prison, but He did not do the same for John the Baptist. In the Old Testament, by faith, some crossed the Red Sea and, through faith, others died.

Until Jesus returns to earth, no miracle is truly completed. If a person is healed of brain cancer, he or she may still be subject to headaches and, of course, he or she will eventually die. We all face the deterioration of the body, a result of the Fall and its curse. Our skin will wrinkle, our hair will turn gray, our bones will weaken with age.

THE GLORY OF GOD

The final issue is, How, by faith, can we seek to see God glorified?

The Christian or cult member who develops a set of expectations excluding either side of the total picture makes improper demands on God, on others, on oneself. That person makes his or her own self the law and thereby judges others, fails to express compassion, and falls into the sin of pride and idolatry.

An acquaintance of mine was dying of terminal cancer. For weeks, even months, the church to which he belonged prayed that God would heal him. But God chose not to intervene. In the midst of his suffering this young man's desire was to glorify Christ. Like Job's comforters, some Christians told him that he must have some secret sin. His parents carried heavy, embarrassed guilt for lacking faith. Yet their accusers never placed such platitudes on themselves.

I will never forget the words that cascaded from this friend's lips after a series of bombarding, accusing questions. He answered his accusers with great confidence, "God has been very good to me. I know I will be leaving this life soon. I know my date. My house is in order; I am ready to meet Jesus Christ face to face. Maybe you should pray for yourselves. You forget that you are terminal also. You just don't know your date."

Although his body was being destroyed, his perspective had been healed. Without the basic foundation of seeking to glorify God, we will lose perspective, live under unnecessary guilt, and be most susceptible to cultic groups. The desire to "glorify God in our bodies" will protect us, inoculate us against the poison of cults that stretch one part of God's truth to encompass the whole of their reality.

> Yes, and I will continue to rejoice, for I know that through your prayers and the help given by the Spirit of Jesus Christ, what has happened to me will turn out for my deliverance. I eagerly expect and hope that I will in no way be ashamed, but will have sufficient courage so that now as always Christ will be exalted in my body, whether by life or by death. For to me, to live is Christ and to die is gain. If I am to go on living in the body, this will mean fruitful labor for me. Yet what shall I choose? I do not know! I am torn between the two: I desire to depart and be with Christ, which is better by far; but it is more necessary for you that I remain in the body. Convinced of this, I know that I will remain, and I will continue with all of you for your progress and joy in the faith, so that through my being with you again your joy in Christ Jesus will overflow on account of me (Phil. 1:18–26).

When he wrote these words, Paul was facing possible martyrdom. He did not condemn the Philippians for not "claiming faith" for his release. Paul only sought to glorify Jesus Christ.

QUESTIONS FOR DISCUSSION

1. Do you agree or disagree with the statement "All miracles are only temporary until Jesus returns"? Why or why not?
2. What are your reactions to the four causes of suffering as presented in this chapter?
3. Do you see any relationship between Habakkuk's words and Paul's?

> Though the fig tree does not bud
> and there are no grapes on the vines,
> though the olive crop fails
> and the fields produce no food,
> though there are no sheep in the pen
> and no cattle in the stalls,
> yet I will rejoice in the LORD,
> I will be joyful in God my Savior.
> The Sovereign LORD is my strength (Hab. 3:17–19).

> For I am convinced that neither death nor life, neither angels nor demons, neither the present nor the future, . . . nor anything else in all creation, will be able to separate us from the love of God that is in Christ Jesus our Lord (Rom. 8:38–39).

4. Read Hebrews 11:32–40 and notice that "by faith" for some involved many negative experiences. Has this chapter helped you understand why?

Chapter 9

The Many Paths
to Spirituality

Many people describe our age as "apocalyptic"—an age in which everything will fall apart, a generation with no hope. We are disillusioned by the floods of corruption in government, economic crisis, religious shallowness, and superficial relationships. When floods of chaos engulf a society, when everything seems to be falling apart, people crave personal security. They are tempted to jump into any lifeboat that might keep them afloat.

Our generation is marked by broken families, abuse of minorities and the elderly and children, pressures of inflation, drugs, and the nuclear potential to annihilate all humanity. Seeing these raging waters, people attempt to cope by relating only to those they are sure of and understand.

At some time, we all fear the future. Among the couples I counsel for marriage, some have firmly decided not to have children. I always ask them why. Their main concern is always something deeper than overpopulation or the hunger crisis, but it is always based on a fear of the future. The thought of having children, spawning a future generation, forces us to crystallize our long-term hopes and goals.

The need for inner peace amid a fear of the future can drive people to the door of cults that offer immediate security, instant answers, support, and compassion.

Peter Marin has dubbed our times the age of the "new narcissism," a generation consumed in self-love. Speaking of a particular psychological cult, he states, "It is all so simple and straightforward. It has the terrifying symplicity of the lobotomized mind: all complexity gone, and in its place the warm wind of forced simplicity blowing away the tab ends of conscience and shame."[1]

Though blessed with tremendous affluence our Western culture is bankrupt in terms of the human relationships God ordained for the purpose of carrying us through life's difficulties. What does the increased enrollment in classes on communication skills and counseling as a profession tell us about our society? People long for relationships that will fill their needs for security and continuity. When this relational bankruptcy is coupled with the overstimulation of our emotions by the media, we become walking emotional vacuums, desperate for something or someone who will fill our void. Immediate self-fulfillment, whether through est, the occult, Eastern religions, or some other cult becomes all-important. These groups seek to meet legitimate needs of an unglued age. They offer new experiences, simplistic answers, meaningful encounters with other people, and an instantaneous structure for life.

CULTURAL BAGGAGE

The struggles of the culture as a whole become a part of each of us. We as Christians cannot help but drag the baggage of the 1980s into our expectations of the church. The shallowness of life, the fear, and the call for immediate fulfillment are diseases that infect us all to some degree. Without knowing it, we may seek to fill the void and heal the disease of our age by trendy programs that give us a sense of meaning.

Instead of seeking renewal for our minds, we often seek to patch them up by dividing life into small, easily defined compartments that we label "spiritual." Like many cult members, we long for simple "how-to" teachings on prayer, worship, evangelism, missions, social service, and family life. The final product: Christians running from speaker to seminar, looking for something to fill the hole in the center of their Being.

When the inevitable pressures of life bear down on us, we are tempted to walk away discouraged or opt for a utopian land where we can cope. In their book *Being Human: The Nature of Spiritual Experience,* Ranald Macaulay and Jerram Barrs point out that two false views of spirituality have influenced the church throughout history. These teachings have led many into false religions and cults.

First, they describe the materialist view. Ours is a materialistic culture,

> a culture which denies the reality of God's existence. Because it denies the existence of God, it allows no possibility of the supernatural working in this world. There can be no relationship with God in the present, though psychological techniques may be used to try to give reality a "religious dimension."[2]

Unfortunately, many Christians unconsciously think this way. For all practical purposes, they live as if they were atheists. How? By failing to ask what difference the existence of God makes in the way they handle finances, make decisions on the job, face moral issues, and order the overall agenda of their lives. Consider: Do you expect God to intervene in your life daily? What difference does your belief in God make in the way you deal with other people, figure your income taxes, solve your problems, or treat people who are different from you?

When we fail to ask continually these basic questions, we start viewing prayer as only a psychological exercise by which we look for instant relief. "Practical atheism" is a subtle deception that can make us vulnerable to the many cults that define religious experience only in terms of psychological phenomena. They offer emotional help, but discount the presence of God in the daily workings of our lives.

PLATONISM

The other false view of spirituality that has influenced many Christian groups and most cults is Platonism.

> In platonic thought the spiritual realm is considered superior to the material. The spirit is housed in a body of clay from which it longs to be released. Death gives that final release. In this life, however, the aim is

to dwell in the realm of the spirit as far as possible . . . and deemphasize and devalue the material realm.[3]

Macaulay and Barrs explain this view and its consequences. From the time of Christ to today, Platonism has had tremendous influence in the church. It is the core of the basic beliefs and teachings of most cults.

What did Plato teach? Basically, that the body is bad and the spirit good. Both the biblical and the Platonic views are different from the materialist view, which denies the spiritual realms of reality. But biblical Christianity differs from Platonism in that Christianity does not present the body as a prison of the immortal soul.

The Bible begins by stating that Someone existed before the Creation. This Person, God, is the all-powerful, sovereign sustainer of the universe. God created the material world and saw it as being good, not a prison. Human beings are created in the image of the Creator. All that God created was good and perfect. At a certain point in history, humanity chose to rebel against God. This revolt did not change the faculties of humanness. People are still rational and reasonable, but they pollute these faculties. People are still aesthetic; they still enjoy beauty. They can still experience and enjoy love, but this, like every other aspect of life on earth, is marred by the effects of the revolt.

In the Bible, redemption is seen in light of creation. Unfortunately some views of Christian growth and spirituality neglect this biblical foundation. As a result they teach a concept of spirituality similar to that of the cults. Ask yourself, What are Christians being redeemed from? Many Christians are asserting and living a denial of life rather than an affirmation of life as God created life to be lived.

The Bible teaches the resurrection of the body, not the immortality of the soul. The Bible places a high value on creation. Jesus Christ became *flesh*. Christ ate and slept, and He bled when His hands were pierced. He experienced all the aspects of being physical, as God so intends for all of us.

The Platonic view of spirituality held by many cults and some Christians sees redemption as *only* a "spiritual" problem. The concept is a subtle one. How often have you said, "Jesus wants to come into your hearts"? Do you think in terms of Jesus saving only "souls"? If so, you may have adopted a cultic concept. The Bible teaches that Jesus Christ wants people in totality—a person's body, family life, thoughts, relationships with others and with the state and with the church. Every aspect of living in our bodies is to be lived before God in thanksgiving. God's plan of redemption is not just futuristic, but includes the process of redemption now.

This is portrayed clearly by Paul in his letter to Christians in Rome. For eleven chapters Paul focuses on doctrine: God's sovereign grace, humanity's sinfulness, and Christ's redeeming work in history. Just before Paul goes on to discuss Christian living (ethics), he uses the word *bodies*.

> Therefore, I urge you, brothers, in view of God's mercy, to offer your bodies as living sacrifices, holy and pleasing to God—which is your spiritual worship. Do not conform any longer to the pattern of this world, but be transformed by the renewing of your mind. Then you will be able to test and approve what God's will is—his good, pleasing and perfect will (Rom. 12:1–2).

Paul reminds us here of the mercy of God. In this context Paul uses this first-century "nonreligious" word *body*. Paul asks these Christians to present their total selves—not just their "hearts" or spirits—to God as a living sacrifice.

Sacrifices were common to the great mystery religions and to Old Testament believers. All these sacrifices involved the killing of a body, but Paul says God wants a living body.

Religious people love to give spiritual sacrifices to win God's favor. But spiritual ecstasy is the only reward for giving only of one's inner self. Fighting the false religions of his day, Paul defines spirituality in terms of our presenting our total selves, including our bodies, to God.

First Corinthians 6:20 tells us to honor God with our bodies. Paul uses this term "body" to refer, in positive terms, to the total person. In much the same manner he uses the term "flesh" (KJV) or "sinful nature" (NIV) to symbolize, in negative terms, our sinful nature (Rom. 8:5).

The Platonic view calls people to be "spiritual." It sounds

right, but how does it differ from the biblical view? The Bible
insists that our problem is moral rebellion against God. For
the Christian, salvation is not a denial of one's humanity, but
a recognition of sin and acceptance of Jesus Christ as one's
Savior. This acceptance enables us to glorify God in our
bodies, as intended before the Fall. The final goal, then, is to
live now under the authority of God's Word, free from guilt,
redeeming all of life.

The Bible views the body in a positive way. Regrettably,
many Christians view the body as distasteful, unspiritual, and
something to be rejected. Such a view of spirituality is similar
to many major cults.

> Ultimately we hope to overcome our bodies or escape them; then we
> will be like Christ, we think. In this view bodily pleasure is especially
> suspect. . . . Sleeping, eating, drinking, going to the bathroom, making
> love, combing our hair, and putting on make-up may be the activity of
> bodies, and may consume a good portion of our day, but these activities
> are seen as irrelevant to or a hindrance to seeking first the kingdom of
> God.[4]

Paul says that if we want to do something religious or spiritual, we should give our bodies to God. The spiritual act will
not be the burning of incense, the pinching of salt, the waiting
for a line-up of the planets, or a searching for the right mood.
It will simply be the presenting of one's entire self to God,
giving back to Him what He gave us in creation.

Biblical spirituality and Christian worship begin with this
act. The Platonists and the cults of the first century would
have viewed Romans 12:1–2 as anti-religious, distasteful, and
unspiritual. So far as they were concerned, the body was evil
and God wanted nothing to do with it. For them the call was
to get out of body and mind and into the spirit.

The great mystery of the Christian faith is the Incarnation,
God becoming flesh, having hinged thumbs and toes, ex-
panding lungs, a valved heart, and a digestive system, God as
man being crucified and then restored in the Resurrection.

> In the beginning was the Word, and the Word was with God, and the
> Word was God. He was with God in the beginning. Through him all
> things were made; without him nothing was made that has been made.

In him was life, and that life was the light of men. The light shines in the darkness, but the darkness has not understood it. . . .

He was in the world, and though the world was made through him, the world did not recognize him. He came to that which was his own, but his own did not receive him. Yet to all who received him, to those who believed in his name, he gave the right to become children of God—children born not of natural descent, nor of human decision or a husband's will, but born of God.

The Word became flesh and lived for a while among us. We have seen his glory, the glory of the one and only Son, who came from the Father, full of grace and truth (John 1:1–5, 10–14).

Jesus Christ, the Word, was raised from the dead; a physical, material being was lifted into the Godhead. If we depreciate our bodies, we depreciate the very vehicle God uses to accomplish His work, which is our sanctification (our becoming more Christlike in character) and our service to others. In an article, "Any Body Can be Spiritual," Bert H. Hodges writes,

The Incarnation was a very physical affair. It involved the birth of a baby. . . . Jesus went to a wedding . . . touched people . . . healed their sicknesses . . . ate meals. . . .

The physicalness of the Incarnation is so blatant that it embarrasses us as "spiritual" Christians. We wish the Incarnation were somehow a more pristine, mystical affair. That God became body and lived in this mundane, fallen world where one must be concerned with dressing, eating, sleeping, sexuality and the effects of sin on these activities is too mysterious.[5]

Paul saw the giving of our bodies as the apex of spirituality. Why? So that we might test, through experience, the will of God. In this aspect, the will of God is the same for all. "Spiritual worship," the giving of our bodies and minds, is the key to discovering that God's will is good, squares with reality, is acceptable, and brings maturity and wholeness. God's will is not some nebulous mystical formula; it involves giving our minds and bodies to God so that we can live to God's glory.

The apostle uses the language of laypeople and amateurs. Those who speak religious expert-ese would cringe at the use of the words *bodies* and *minds*, but these two words should not be taken lightly. The body and mind are the focal point of the Book of Romans, the transition between doctrine (teaching) and practice (living). The rest of Paul's letter gives instruction regarding one's responsibility to family, neighbors, and the state.

Paul doesn't say, "Give yourselves when you become holy." Neither does he ask believers to present their hearts, souls, or spirits to God—that would be too easy! He says we must give our created, concrete selves, with all their fears, doubts, problems, abilities, gifts, dreams, and hopes. Give your problematic self to God. That is spirituality.

NOT ALL BLISS

Lest we be naïve, we must note that Paul informs believers of an immediate crisis: There will be a tension between the passing idols of each age and God's values (Rom. 12:2). This tension cannot be avoided, regardless of how "spiritual" we may become. Paul urges believers to call the bluff of all such fads.

This concept of spirituality will greatly influence whether we confront or run from the various crises brought by living in a world affected by the Fall.

Faith in this context is a good discovery. Faith does not negate our humanity. It is, in the words of Ranald Macaulay and Jerram Barrs, an "affirmation of life." To be human is to be in the image of God.

Paul says that God's love triggers our faith. False religions and cults claim that our increased faith will increase God's love for us, but actually our faith does not influence God's love. Because of God's mercy, love, and grace, we can and should trust Jesus Christ with our total being. When we keep this foremost in our minds, we are immune to the false teaching that only certain people can be spiritual.

Giving one's total self is essential to understanding and discerning the deception and bluff of cults.

WHY RENEW THE MIND?

We must not assume that only pastors, leaders, or counselors can have renewed minds. The Holy Spirit can renew any believer's mind in concrete ways.

A renewed mind is critical for discerning false teaching in the church and in cults. Many Christians are calling for us to get out of the mind and into the spirit, but doing so may prove dangerous. This aspect of our humanity is God's major weapon to protect us from false teachings and cults.

In his book *Your Mind Matters,* John R. W. Stott states, "Nobody wants a cold, joyless, intellectual Christianity."[6] How true! But Stott explains that a Christian's battle against the forces of evil is a battle of the mind, a battle of ideas.

Note Paul's references to maturity, discernment, and Christian living in the following passages. They are found in a mind when Jesus Christ is its Lord.

> The weapons we fight with are not the weapons of the world. On the contrary, they have divine power to demolish strongholds. We demolish arguments and every pretension that sets itself up against the knowledge of God, and we take captive every thought to make it obedient to Christ. And we will be ready to punish every act of disobedience, once your obedience is complete (2 Cor. 10:4–6).

> Finally, brothers, whatever is true, whatever is noble, whatever is right, whatever is pure, whatever is lovely, whatever is admirable—if anything is excellent or praiseworthy—think about such things. Whatever you have learned or received or heard from me, or seen in me—put it into practice. And the God of peace will be with you (Phil. 4:8–9).

Both passages say our thoughts—our renewed minds—safeguard us against deception. A mind "not renewed" is a mind vulnerable to cults and false teaching.

HOW DO WE JUDGE A FALSE TEACHER?

How are we to judge prophets? On the spiritual feeling we receive in our spirits? No! On the content of their message.

> The Spirit clearly says that in later times some will abandon the faith and follow deceiving spirits and things taught by demons. Such teachings come through hypocritical liars, whose consciences have been seared as with a hot iron. They forbid people to marry and order them to abstain from certain foods, which God created to be received with thanksgiving by those who believe and who know the truth (1 Tim. 4:1–4).

False teachers, even those who call themselves Christians, will always despise creation. They will present a higher, legalistic spirituality. Creation for the believer has been sanctified and consecrated by God; it is to be received with gratitude. Note Paul's words: "For everything God created is good, and nothing is to be rejected if it is received with thanksgiving, because it is consecrated by the word of God and prayer" (1 Tim. 4:4–5).

John also warns the church of false teachers. Does he encourage them to judge a teacher by the feelings of spirituality given off? No. Again, our minds must examine the content of a teacher's message, noticing what is said about Jesus Christ having come in a body.

> Dear friends, do not believe every spirit, but test the spirits to see whether they are from God, because many false prophets have gone out into the world. This is how you can recognize the Spirit of God: Every spirit that acknowledges that Jesus Christ has come in the flesh is from God, but every spirit that does not acknowledge Jesus is not from God. This is the spirit of the antichrist, which you have heard is coming and even now is already in the world (1 John 4:1–3).

To judge the spirituality of pastors, speakers, Sunday school teachers, and evangelists on the amount of emotion they exude or stir up is wrong and dangerous. The movie *Deceived* recalls many People's Temple services in which persons shared needs, gave testimonies, and praised God with great excitement. But they were deceived; the depth of their emotion and excitement was not founded in the discovery of God's love through Jesus Christ. The knowledge of Christ will lead to true worship, faith, holiness, and love (see Rom. 11:33; Luke 24:32; John 13:17).

The Holy Spirit *can* renew anyone's mind. A Ph.D. is not a prerequisite for being able to discern and thus be protected from deception. A mind renewed by God's Spirit and the knowledge of His Word is available to all believers who concern themselves with prayer, faith, study, reflection, and personal commitment to Christ's lordship. The minds given to us by God in creation are integral and crucial to our spirituality. Minds renewed are minds protected from deception, fraud, and manipulation. If in our minds we think we are not susceptible to cults, we are most vulnerable.

QUESTIONS FOR DISCUSSION

1. What issues has this chapter raised in your thinking?
2. What is your response to the following statement: "If the words *body* and *minds* sound unspiritual to you, you may be closer to cults in your thinking than you realize."
3. Do you see any platonic overtones in your concepts of spirituality?
4. Has this chapter helped you to understand the meaning of Paul's words in Philippians 4:8–9? If so, how?

> Finally, brothers, whatever is true, whatever is noble, whatever is right, whatever is pure, whatever is lovely, whatever is admirable—if anything is excellent or praiseworthy—think about such things. Whatever you have learned or received or heard from me, or seen in me—put it into practice. And the God of peace will be with you.

5. Do you confuse being sinful with being human? What are your reactions to the following statement: "Jesus Christ came to negate our sin, not our humanity."

Chapter 10

Please Don't Water
the Garden

A Boston television station produced a series of programs
on the land of Egypt and its history. One of these programs
focused on the treasures discovered in the ancient tombs.
Among these finds were some grains of wheat. The archaeol-
ogists planted these seeds, which had been entombed for several thousand years, in rich soil. They were watered and given
sunlight, and to everyone's amazement, they grew.

Christians often think that the seeds of heresy are found
only in cults and in off-beat sects of Christianity. But John, in
his first letter, and Paul, in his letter to the Ephesians, remind
us that heretical teachers are often found within the church
itself. Jesus notes that the dormant seeds of heresy can be
buried in the lawns of the church. In Matthew 13, Jesus tells a
parable of the kingdom of heaven: The enemy sowed seeds
within this kingdom. In our desire to discover and understand
the doctrines of cults, we may forget that potential gardens of
heresy lie within our own walls. Remember: Sun Myung
Moon was raised a Presbyterian; David Berg, founder of the
Children of God, was once an Evangelical pastor; Jim Jones
pastored a Christian church; many leaders in the People's
Temple and Jonestown were former members of Nazarene,
Roman Catholic, Baptist, Methodist, and Assemblies of God
churches.

Under the right circumstances we are all capable of watering the seeds of heresy that lie dormant in the church itself. Without even realizing what they are doing, pastors can water these gardens. Congregations can unwittingly build greenhouses. Parachurch organizations can make the "spring rains" fall. And individuals can add the nutrients that cause these plants to flourish and ripen, ready for harvest.

HOW CAN PASTORS WATER THE GARDEN?

Pastors can water the seedbeds of heresy by projecting the image that their lives are all-together and free from struggles and weaknesses. When this happens, they invite unhealthy loyalties into the congregation.

God often matches congregations with pastors for mutual ministry. The word *ministry* implies giving help. Mutual ministry implies that both the pastor and the congregation have needs to be met by the other. The congregation may be strong in qualities where the pastor is weak, and vice versa. This kind of ministry of growth involves continual self-evaluation, prayer, thought, and serious study of God's Word. A constant willingness by both pastor and congregation to be open to instruction —from God's Word, from mutual confrontation, and from prayer for each other—will deter exploitation.

Pastors water the seeds of heresy when they spend the majority of their time in administration rather than in consistent Bible study and in ministry to their congregations. Pastors may encourage congregations to build unhealthy images of the pastoral ministry when they live as though their "higher calling" is free from struggle and weaknesses.

Pastors and leaders need to know their personal limitations. There is a danger in confusing the role of pastor with that of a professional counselor. Counseling demands have led many pastors to exhaustion; with only twenty-four hours in the day, they have had to lower the quality of their teaching and preaching. Some have become so discouraged, they have left the ministry. A pastor's primary call is to teach God's Word and to minister to the congregation. Of course, this will involve some counseling; involvement with and concern for people's needs must not be avoided, for this was the model of Christ. But not admitting our counseling limitations can produce some tragic results. We may create an unhealthy dependence for members of our congregation, which may further result in unhealthy and misaligned affections.

Personally I see the need to protect myself from long-term counseling relationships. As a rule, I allow only four counseling sessions per problem. After four sessions I evaluate the situation and decide: Will I continue, or direct the person to professional help? This gives me freedom to place checks and balances on myself and avoid unhealthy emotional attachments or dependencies. At this juncture I often direct the person to a Bible study group or another group designed to meet his or her specific need. This evaluation point also protects me from yielding to any temptation to meet my own egoistic needs by building unhealthy cultic-type loyalties.

As pastors we can also water the seeds of heresy when we fail to keep in mind the biblical goals of discipling. Our goal should be to help move those who look to us for guidance toward growth and development that is separate from us. The Book of Acts presents a unique picture of a healthy, helping, discipling relationship. Soon after Paul's conversion, Barnabas took Paul under his care, helping him to develop as a church leader. The first references to the pair speak of "Barnabas and Paul." But later the writer of Acts shifts the relationship to "Paul and Barnabas," and eventually the focus is only on Paul. We water heretical seeds when we fail to encourage those under our care to continue their development, perhaps even beyond our own.

This model of discipling and shepherding is unique, healthful, and successful. Barnabas was concerned that Paul develop his own skills, style, and abilities, that he move out of a dependent relationship into a more personally fulfilled ministry.

CHURCHES CAN BUILD GREENHOUSES

Without even realizing it, Christian churches can build the walls of a greenhouse in which cultic tendencies flourish, in which seedlings sprout, and from where they can be transplanted into someone else's garden. What material do we use for the studs and beams of these greenhouses? What kind of solar panels do we use? What auxiliary heat do we employ?

We pour the foundation and put up the studs when we build a total ministry around one personality. There should be a sense of excitement about what God is doing in many American "superchurches." Many of these large congregations enjoy continuing growth and creative ministries. But a pattern shared by many of these churches needs to be checked: At first the pastor preaches good sermons with good biblical exegesis, causing crowds to come. Before long, the church hosts a nationwide radio program, a cassette ministry, and perhaps a television ministry. The pastor is soon marketed Madison Avenue-style, and in time the superchurch becomes marked with its own trendy clichés. Often the demands of the pastorate become so great that sermon content begins to take second place to other responsibilities.

Listen to the message presented in your church. Be ever grateful for what God has accomplished, but ask yourself whether, over the years, biblical content has given way to stories or fads of the decade. Take a pen and paper and note the amount of time spent on raising money, dealing with issues, story-telling, and solid biblical instruction with practical application.

Congregations build these greenhouses when they allow themselves to be enamored by success without ever examining the possible subtle flaws in the church structure.

We water the little seeds of heresy in new converts when we continually talk about the pastor rather than about Jesus Christ. These seeds can easily sprout and then be transplanted into another garden, maybe that of some new personality cult.

Churches install the solar panels and lights that encourage the growth of heresy when their ministry is centered around only one aspect of the gospel, thus neglecting the whole counsel of God. They might teach only the ministry of the Holy Spirit or evangelism or missions or body-life or prophecy. A fragmented perspective on Scripture will nourish the dormant seeds that lie waiting for conditions conducive to life. In this kind of church, members are often not free to discern from the whole counsel of God, the preaching of which would help entomb heresy.

We nourish false teaching when we have unrealistic and unbiblical expectations of what the church should be. We nourish the sprouts of heresy when we get more excited about hearing stories than about the biblical truths they illustrate.

Congregations are often guilty of putting their pastors in a bind, expecting them to spend a majority of time in administration rather than in ministry or Bible study. Such unbiblical demands can cause the best of pastors to veer off track, to succumb to unbiblical priorities.

ORGANIZATIONS THAT WATER THE SOIL

During the past few decades, many parachurch ministries have been born. They have been responsible for the conversion of many, yet are all these groups really just an arm of the church, as they claim? Many pastors who have worked close to the central offices of parachurch organizations can tell a string of tragic stories about burned-out leaders and the rubble of the families of those who have given their lives for the cause. They can describe families who are not involved in a local church because of the pressures of their ministry.

We need to ask ourselves: Are the parachurch ministries really a functioning arm of the church or an arm severed? To whom are such organizations accountable? When we accept their ministries without questioning their accountability, their view of the church, or their handling of finances, we prepare the way for seeds of deception to grow.

Parachurch organizations, including what is called the "electronic church," water the seeds of heresy when they define themselves in opposition to the local church, all the while coaxing (without accountability) money from the local church members.

On one occasion I was invited by a national parachurch youth organization to speak at a high school. The speaker before me spent fifteen minutes explaining how his organization, disillusioned with the church, identified with the student's rejection of the institution. I was then introduced as a pastor from a local church! These incongruous messages cannot help but confuse the people who hear them. Such messages turn people against the very institution God ordained to be their help. I felt compelled to discuss my reactions with the speaker. I thank God we agreed to help each other's ministry. Our parish developed a training program for their leaders, and they directed new converts to us to become established in a local church.

Another problem is that a parachurch organization can be orthodox in doctrine, yet function like a cult in issues of authority and abuse of power.

While living in Europe, my wife and I were involved with an Evangelical youth mission based in Switzerland. We were with the group only six weeks, but it was almost seven years before I had overcome the psychological damage caused by their cult-like control and spiritualization.

Upon arrival at the headquarters each team member was given a "victory sheet," which instructed him or her never to question those in leadership and never to write home any negative comments. Questioning a leader was considered an act of rebellion against God and His chain of command. Team members were kept constantly busy, even overextended, for the cause. Married partners were separated from each other. All the organization's demands were adhered to for the sake of "spirituality." When some of us grew tired, causing tempers to shrink, those in authority pointed out how sinful we were and how much we needed to depend on those in spiritual authority over us. Any of us who raised questions regarding the stewardship of our bodies were suddenly branded as being "in the flesh." Any who questioned exaggerated stories of miracles, finances, or poor diets were accused of bringing sin into the camp.

When I think of this group and other parachurch groups who value authority and uniformity, I recall the words of Ronald Enroth:

> In strongly authoritarian movements or churches, those who persist in raising uncomfortable questions, especially after they have left the group, are labeled "reprobates" or worse yet, "agents of Satan." The weak and the meek who have legitimate concerns and questions do not dare to share those reservations, sometimes because of group pressure, sometimes because they have been subjected to control mechanisms of fear, guilt, and spiritual intimidation.[1]

Although the group I was in was thoroughly Christian in doctrine and in motive, they were blind to the manipulative controls being placed on team members. How tragic that some who left the team have rejected not only the parachurch organization, but the church and Christ. They still have not fully recovered.

We need to remember that people who have been burned by questionable tactics of a parachurch group or a church may heal *very* slowly. This is pointed out by James and Marcia Rudin in their book *Prison or Paradise?;* they show that it can take years to overcome the fears and psychological damage incurred in a cultic group. Personal experience has shown me that it can take years for a victim to stabilize, learn to trust others, and to build healthy relationships. People often need professional help beyond what a pastor or church is able to give.

Parachurch organizations can sow dishonesty when they use tricky means to hide their evangelistic agendas. Questions about integrity should be asked when evangelism campaigns are launched under the guise of "church surveys." What is the difference between these surveys and the computerized surveys used by some of the leading cults to lure converts? Surely there is no difference in tactic.

Parachurch groups cultivate the seeds of cultism and heresy when they claim to offer more than the church rather than claiming to be a supporting arm of the church. I recently attended a meeting of Christians where the speaker was the host of a popular Christian television talk program. I took note of one particular sentence: "Most church services are boring and most TV church services are boring." Immediately the audience broke into applause. In a sense, they

were applauding the seeds of heresy. They were revealing their misunderstanding of the nature, purpose, and mission of the church and worship. We reveal our worldliness when we come to church expecting worship to be another "Sesame Street" explosion of entertainment. When we rate a worship service only on its level of excitement, we border on being deceived by the bizarre—that which will delight, dazzle, and entertain. The services of the People's Temple were characterized by joyful, excited expressions of testimony and songs of praise; their delight had nothing to do with true Christianity.

Certainly the discipline of going to worship can be boring. Weekly confession of our sins to God can also be boring. Who like to get on their knees and worship God or discipline their minds to hear God's Word or acknowledge that God only is God? We make the ground ready for cult leaders to sow the seeds of heresy when we follow the world in thinking that life, including worship, should be all thrills.

WEED KILLER ALONE WILL NOT DO THE JOB

There will always be some seeds of heresy lying buried in the church. We are deceived if we think that right doctrine alone is the weed killer that will destroy them forever.

John, the beloved disciple, addressed this problem in his writings to the early church. John was with Christ throughout His ministry. They were close friends. Jesus entrusted His mother to John's care. John witnessed the birth of the church and was one of its founding leaders. But at the close of his life, wrinkled by age, John saw the need to challenge the seeds of heresy within the church. Note the power of his words:

> Dear children, this is the last hour; and as you have heard that the antichrist is coming, even now many antichrists have come. This is how we know it is the last hour. They went out from us, but they did not really belong to us. For if they had belonged to us, they would have remained with us; but their going showed that none of them belonged to us.

> But you have an anointing from the Holy One, and all of you know the truth. I do not write to you because you do not know the truth, but because you do know it and because no lie comes from the truth. Who is the liar? It is the man who denies that Jesus is the Christ. Such a man is the antichrist—he denies the Father and the Son (1 John 2:18–22).

The ultimate deceiver, the ultimate cult leader, will be the Antichrist, but this letter was written to Christians, not to members of some crazy cult. John makes it clear that the seeds of heresy are in *our* hearts. When we deny that Jesus Christ is Lord we are, in spirit, the Antichrist.

When do we deny Christ? When we willfully continue to do what we know is wrong. Seeds of heresy are nourished when we willfully harbor bitterness, prejudice, and an unforgiving spirit. We may be doctrinally sound, but if we in practice willfully reject God's Word, we deny Christ. So John continues his letter by encouraging us to practice the Christian life.

Many people never lose their faith—they just fail to shape their lives by it. Behavior unchecked, attitudes not dealt with, resentments harbored—all cause us to build up beliefs that justify our immaturity and irresponsible behavior.

Even after having several children, husbands or wives have told me that their marriages were "out of the will of God" and therefore they were going to leave their families. I even listened as one woman told me that after much prayer, the Holy Spirit had led her to Paul's words, "Put on the new man." She took the "word" as telling her to leave her husband for someone else. Though this particular situation is extreme, isn't it, in principle, how we rationalize many of our actions? John continues his instruction in his letter by listing safeguards that protect us from this subtle deception. John's counsel can be summarized in two words: obedience and service.

> And now, dear children, continue in him, so that when he appears we may be confident and unashamed before him at his coming.
>
> If you know that he is righteous, you know that everyone who does what is right has been born of him.
>
> How great is the love the Father has lavished on us, that we should be called children of God! And that is what we are! The reason the world does not know us is that it did not know him. Dear friends, now we are children of God, and what we will be has not yet been made known. But we know that when he appears, we shall be like him, for we shall see him as he is. Everyone who has this hope in him purifies himself, just as he is pure.

> Everyone who sins breaks the law; in fact, sin is lawlessness. But you know that he appeared so that he might take away our sins. And in him is no sin. No one who lives in him keeps on sinning. No one who continues to sin has either seen him or known him.
>
> Dear children, do not let anyone lead you astray. He who does what is right is righteous, just as he is righteous. He who does what is sinful is of the devil, because the devil has been sinning from the beginning. The reason the Son of God appeared was to destroy the devil's work. No one who is born of God will continue to sin, because God's seed remains in him; he cannot go on sinning, because he has been born of God. This is how we know who the children of God are and who the children of the devil are: Anyone who does not do what is right is not a child of God; neither is anyone who does not love his brother (1 John 2:28–3:10).

If we are to be alert to these issues of self-deception and manipulation by others—the pitfalls of denying Christ—we must earnestly pray, study the Word, examine ourselves, and honestly reflect upon the whole counsel of God. We need to know both our strengths and our weaknesses. We must guard those areas where we know we are most tempted to manipulate others or to allow them to manipulate us. We are all sinful. To think otherwise is to deceive ourselves. Remember that the warning "If we claim to be without sin, we deceive ourselves and the truth is not in us" (1 John 1:8) was written to Christians.

Each of us must examine past relationships and see whether there have been certain patterns of behavior and needs that have caused us to use others or allowed them to exploit us. We must stand against those weaknesses and pray with others that God will protect us in the future from such pitfalls.

There is something more dangerous in life than being wrong: being right. When fighting for truth and against cults, we can easily be blind to our own sin. In this blindness we attack the colossal and scandalous faults and mistakes of others without routing our own sins that are just as big and ugly. God's grace frees us to be open with Him and to install checks and balances in our lives. When we place such controls on ourselves, we are less apt to place controls on others.

Apart from Christology, John's letter concerning heresy says little about the nature and teaching of false teachers. He

did remind those first-century believers, and Christians throughout history, that we can all play an unwitting part in allowing the seeds of heresy to grow; we can all plow the ground, plant the seeds, nourish them, build a hothouse, or prepare the sprouts for transplanting.

This old man, this friend of Christ, was concerned that the seeds remain as dormant as those wheat seeds that were sealed inside the Egyptian pyramid. John was concerned that none of us be guilty of watering the garden.

QUESTIONS FOR DISCUSSION

1. Have you ever been involved in a Christian church or fellowship group that was marked by cultic tendencies?
2. Have the issues raised in this book helped you in any way? Which chapters have been most helpful? least helpful? Why?
3. Do you agree or disagree with the author's interpretation of 1 John 2:22–23?

   > It is the man who denies that Jesus is the Christ. Such a man is the antichrist—he denies the Father and the Son.

4. In which ways, thought and deed, do you deny Christ?

Notes

CHAPTER 1

[1]John Moriconi, *Children of God, Family of Love* (Downers Grove, Ill.: InterVarsity Press, 1980), 39 pp.

CHAPTER 3

[1]Ronald Enroth, *Youth, Brainwashing and the Extremist Cults* (Grand Rapids: Zondervan, 1977), p. 208.
[2]Ibid., p. 203.
[3]Mel White, *Deceived* (Old Tappan, N.J.: Fleming H. Revell, 1979), p. 231.
[4]Stephen B. Clark, *Man and Woman in Christ* (Ann Arbor, Mich.: Servant Books, 1980), p. 360.
[5]Ibid.
[6]Charles Farah, Jr., "A Critical Analysis: The 'Roots and Fruits' of Faith-Formula Theology," in *Pneuma: The Journal of the Society for Pentecostal Studies* (Spring 1981):15.
[7]See discussion of this in Farah, "A Critical Analysis," p. 17.
[8]A. James Rudin and Marcia R. Rudin, *Prison or Paradise? The New Religious Cults* (Philadelphia: Fortress Press, 1980), p. 23.
[9]Michael Griffiths, *Unsplitting Your Christian Life* (Downers Grove, Ill.: InterVarsity Press, 1971), p. 22.
[10]Ibid., p. 23.
[11]Ibid., p. 25.

CHAPTER 4

[1]"Congressional Report Recommends Actions As Result of Jonestown Tragedy," in *The Advisor: Journal of the American Family Foundation* 1, no. 1 (August 1979):2: Citing the report entitled "The Assassination of Representative Leo T. Ryan and the Jonestown, Guyana Tragedy," U.S. Govt. Printing Office (15 May 1979).

[2]Curtis Hartman, with Ann Rodgers and Tom Morton, "God for the 'Up and Out,'" in *Boston* 73, no. 5 (May 1981):143.

[3]Ibid., p. 188.

CHAPTER 5

[1]Dietrich Bonhoeffer, *Life Together* (New York: Harper & Row, 1954), pp. 27–28.

CHAPTER 6

[1]Lucille Lavender, *They Cry, Too!* (Wheaton, Ill.: Tyndale House Publishers, 1979).

[2]Ronald M. Enroth, "Door Interview," in the *Wittenburg Door* 59 (February-March 1981):14.

[3]Ronald M. Enroth, "The Power Abusers," in *Eternity* (October 1979):23.

[4]Ibid., p. 24.

[5]Paul Tournier, *The Violence Within*, trans. Edwin Hudson (San Francisco: Harper & Row, 1978), p. 148.

[6]Ben Patterson, "Don Quixote and the Cults," Editorial, in the *Wittenburg Door* 59 (February-March 1981):5.

[7]Steven W. Larson, "And a Little Child Shall Lead Them" (Unpublished course text, Gordon College, Wenham, Mass., 1980), p. 23.

CHAPTER 8

[1]James W. Sire, *Scripture Twisting: 20 Ways the Cults Misread the Bible* (Downers Grove, Ill.: InterVarsity Press, 1980). This is one of the best books available for helping Christians to understand a basic approach to biblical interpretation.

[2]Gordon D. Fee, *The Disease of the Health and Wealth Gospels* (Costa Mesa, Calif.: The Word for Today, n.d.). These essays originally appeared in *Agora* magazine in 1979.

CHAPTER 9

[1]Peter Marin, "The New Narcissism," in *Harper's Magazine* (October 1975):46.

[2]Ranald Macaulay and Jerram Barrs, *Being Human: The Nature of Spiritual Experience* (Downers Grove, Ill.: InterVarsity Press, 1978), p. 30.

[3]Ibid., p. 43.

[4]Bert H. Hodges, "Any Body Can Be Spiritual," in the *Gordon Alumnus* 11, no. 1 (Summer 1981):23.

[5]Ibid., pp. 23–24.

[6]John R. W. Stott, *Your Mind Matters: The Place of the Mind in the Christian Life* (Downers Grove, Ill.: InterVarsity Press, 1973), p. 1.

CHAPTER 10

[1]Enroth, "The Power Abusers."

Bibliography

The Advisor: Journal of the American Family Foundation, August 1979.

Augsburger, David. *Caring Enough to Confront.* Glendale, Calif.: Regal Books, 1974.

Berghoef, Gerard, and De Koster, Lester. *The Elders Handbook: A Practical Guide for Church Leaders.* Grand Rapids: Christian's Library Press, 1979.

Bonhoeffer, Dietrich. *Life Together.* New York: Harper & Row, 1954.

Clark, Stephen B. *Man and Woman in Christ.* Ann Arbor: Servant Books, 1980.

Collins, Gary. *People Helper Growthbook.* Santa Ana, Calif.: Vision House, 1979.

Dodds, E. R. *Pagan and Christian in an Age of Anxiety.* New York: W. W. Norton, 1965.

Enroth, Ronald M. "The Power Abusers." *Eternity,* October 1979, p. 22.

_____ . "Door Interview." *Wittenburg Door,* February-March 1981, pp. 14–15.

_____ . *Youth, Brainwashing and the Extremist Cults.* Grand Rapids: Zondervan, 1977.

Farah, Charles, Jr. "A Critical Analysis: The 'Roots and Fruits' of Faith-Formula Theology." *Pneuma: The Journal of the Society for Pentecostal Studies,* Spring 1981, pp. 3–21.

Fee, Gordon D. *The Disease of the Health and Wealth Gospels.* Costa Mesa, Calif.: The Word for Today, n.d.

Griffiths, Michael [...] *Christian Life*. Downers Grove, Ill.: InterVarsity Press, 1971.

Hartman, Curtis et al. "God for the 'Up and Out.'" *Boston,* May 1981, p. 142.

Hodges, Bert H. "Any Body Can Be Spiritual." *Gordon Alumnus,* Summer 1981, pp. 21–24.

Larson, Steven W. "And a Little Child Shall Lead Them: A Brief Study of Power, Leadership, and Servanthood." Unpublished course text, Gordon College, Wenham, Mass., 1980.

Lavender, Lucille. *They Cry, Too!* Wheaton, Ill.: Tyndale House Publishers, 1979.

Macaulay, Ranald, and Barrs, Jerram. *Being Human: The Nature of Spiritual Experience.* Downers Grove, Ill.: InterVarsity Press, 1978.

Marin, Peter. "The New Narcissism." *Harper's Magazine,* October 1975.

Martin, Walter R. *The Kingdom of the Cults.* Rev. ed. Minneapolis: Bethany Fellowship, 1968.

Moriconi, John. *Children of God, Family of Love.* Downers Grove, Ill.: InterVarsity Press, 1980.

Patterson, Ben. "Don Quixote and the Cults." *Wittenburg Door,* February-March 1981, p. 3.

Rudin, A. James, and Rudin, Marcia R. *Prison or Paradise? The New Religious Cults.* Philadelphia: Fortress Press, 1980.

Schaeffer, Edith. *Affliction.* Old Tappan, N.J.: Fleming H. Revell, 1978.

Sire, James W. *Scripture Twisting: 20 Ways the Cults Misread the Bible.* Downers Grove, Ill.: InterVarsity Press, 1980.

Sproul, R. C. *Knowing Scripture.* Downers Grove, Ill.: InterVarsity Press, 1977.

Stedman, Ray C. *Body Life.* Glendale, Calif.: Regal Books, 1972.

Stott, John R. W. *Your Mind Matters: The Place of the Mind in the Christian Life.* Downers Grove, Ill.: InterVarsity Press, 1973.

Tournier, Paul. *The Violence Within.* Translated by Edwin Hudson. San Francisco: Harper & Row, 1978.

White, Mel. *Deceived.* Old Tappan, N.J.: Fleming H. Revell, Spire Books, 1979.

Wise, Robert L. *When There Is No Miracle.* Glendale, Calif.: Regal Books, 1977.

Yamamoto, J. Isamu. *The Moon Doctrine.* 2nd ed. Downers Grove, Ill.: InterVarsity Press, 1977.